DATE DUE

NOV 25 03			
NO 17 03			

Demco, Inc. 38-293

The Kingdom of Love
and the
Pride of Life

by

EDWARD JOHN CARNELL

WILLIAM B. EERDMANS PUBLISHING COMPANY
Grand Rapids, Michigan

Preface

Apologetics is that branch of Christian theology which has the task of defending the faith. "But in your hearts reverence Christ as Lord. Always be prepared to make a defense [an apology] to any one who calls you to account for the hope that is in you, yet do it with gentleness and reverence" (I Peter 3:15).[1] While a Christian should *never* defend himself, he should *always* defend the truth.

There is no "official" or "normative" approach to apologetics. At least I have never found one. The approach is governed by the climate of the times. This means, as it were, that an apologist must play it by ear.

For example, when Augustine faced the charge that Christianity was to be blamed for the sack of Rome, and thus was a hostile religion, he told the Romans to think back on their own national heroes — heroes whose deeds were abundantly recorded in history and everywhere celebrated. These noble Romans were praised for their justice, courage, and temperance, the very virtues that Christians were taught to honor. In other words, Rome was sacked because of its luxury and sin, not because Christianity had taken root on its soil. The noble Romans would bear witness to this truth. "If the famous Scipio Nasica were now alive, who was once your pontiff, and was

[1]The Scripture quotations are from the Revised Standard Version of the Bible, copyrighted 1946 and 1952, and are used by permission of the copyright owners, the Division of Christian Education of the National Council of the Churches of Christ in the U.S.A.

unanimously chosen by the senate, when, in the panic created by the Punic war, they sought for the best citizen to entertain the Phrygian goddess, he would curb this shamelessness of yours, though you would perhaps scarcely dare look upon the countenance of such a man. For why in your calamities do you complain of Christianity, unless because you desire to enjoy your luxurious licence unrestrained, and to lead an abandoned and profligate life without the interruption of any uneasiness or disaster?"[2]

Notice how Augustine proceeded. First, he found a useful point of contact between the gospel and culture. He then went on to argue that if the Romans were consistent in their position, they would *reverence* the name of Christ, not *blaspheme* it; for Christ is the absolute embodiment of whatever relative virtues were celebrated in the national heroes of Rome. I think that Augustine went at things in the right way.

In my own books on apologetics I have consistently tried to build on some useful point of contact between the gospel and culture. In *An Introduction to Christian Apologetics* the appeal was to the law of contradiction; in *A Philosophy of the Christian Religion* it was to values; and in *Christian Commitment* it was to the judicial sentiment. In this book I am appealing to the law of love.

I must confess, however, that I did not appreciate the apologetical significance of love until I read Freud. The more I reflected on the relationship between patient and analyst, the more convinced I became that psychotherapy has unwittingly created a new base for Christian apologetics. Christianity has always defended love as the law of life. A highly respected branch of science now joins forces in this defense. I should say we are living in thrilling days.

Freud taught his patients the art of seeing themselves through their own childhood. He believed that people become anxious,

2*The City of God*, I, 30.

6

and thus lessen their chances of leading happy, normal lives, because somewhere along the line they have lost the natural zest and unconditional faith of childhood.

I think that Jesus would accept this Freudian insight, for he urged his own disciples to imitate the manners of a child. A happy child bears witness to the release that love brings: release from anxiety, fear, and the dread of not counting. A child completes his life through the wisdom and power of those who watch over him. He is not sufficient unto himself, nor does he pretend to be. Jesus says we should go and do likewise. We must learn to rest in the sovereignty of God. The more we try to save ourselves by personal striving, the more we lose ourselves, for no man can transcend the limits that God has written into the creation.

Psychotherapy has shown that every normal person has a restless urge to count. When this urge is gratified, a sense of peace is felt. But when it is frustrated, the ego must prove itself by all sorts of competitive strategies. These strategies are self-defeating, however, for they hinder the work of love. No one likes a person who is always showing off.

Love is an act of unconditional acceptance. It receives another person just as he is, without one plea. It raises no legal barriers; it says, "I accept you, you count." Love is always kind and truthful, and it seeks nothing but kindness and truth in return.

When a person is accepted, he can rest in the green pastures of friendship. He does not have to be on guard. This relief not only kindles a lively sense of hope, but it also helps clarify the more exacting duties of love. Love is immature unless friends are willing to go all the way in trusting each other.

Humility is the key to healing, whether in psychotherapy or in the gospel. A humble person is honest with himself and with others. He resists pretense; he returns to the simplicity of childhood.

Pride hinders the work of healing. It tempts a man to think more highly of himself than he ought, and thus to entertain an

7

arrogance of soul that rejects the ethic of honesty. Pretense may satisfy for a season, but in the end it leaves deposits of loneliness and futility. There is no happiness without love, no love without humility.

No contemporary thinker has made better use of this truth, or come to more surprising conclusions, than Paul Tillich. "You cannot help people who are in psychosomatic distress by telling them what to do. You can help them only by giving them something — by accepting them. This means help through the grace which is active in the healing relationship whether it is done by the minister or by the doctor. This, of course, includes the reformation point of view, a view which has also been rediscovered by medicine, namely, you must feel that you have been accepted. Only then can one accept himself. It is never the other way around. That was the plight of Luther in his struggle against the distorted late Roman Church which wanted 'that men make themselves first acceptable and then God would accept them.' But it is always the other way around. First you must be accepted. Then you can accept yourself, and that means, you can be healed. Illness, in the largest sense of body, soul, and spirit, is estrangement."[3] As Tillich sees things, the gospel is good news because it teaches sinners to say "Yes" in their encounter with anxiety, nothingness, and despair. The healing reality of the New Being in Christ breaks through existential conflicts and overcomes estrangement.

If I understand Tillich correctly, he is attempting to construct an elaborate analogy between human and divine acceptance. This analogy has illuminated many elements in the Christian faith. The church should be sincerely grateful for what Tillich has accomplished.

It seems to me, however, that Tillich speculates more than he exegetes. He patterns the gospel after the manner in which psychotherapists defy convention by accepting the unacceptable, rather than patterning it after what the Bible actually teaches.

[3]*Theology of Culture* (Oxford), p. 211. This citation first appeared in the *Union Seminary Quarterly Review*, VII, 4, June 1952. Used by permission.

I think that this approach surrenders the objective elements in faith. God indeed says, "I accept you," but only because Jesus bore the curse of the law through his death on the cross. If the Father had not been reconciled to the world through the sacrifice of the Son, there would be no gospel, and hence no word of divine forgiveness.

Conservative theologians are persuaded that God has definitively revealed his will in the Bible. Hence, they sense a moral responsibility to pattern their thoughts after this system of revealed truth.

This is good as far as it goes. But conservatives often leap to the conclusion that everything worth knowing is in the Bible. This has the dreadful effect of separating the gospel from culture. Conservatives rarely take leadership in showing how the gospel answers questions which the natural man, in his search for meaning, has already raised about himself and the world. As a result, the natural man concludes that the gospel is irrelevant.

This is why conservatives are not more excited by psychotherapy's defense of love as a necessary ingredient in a happy, integrated life. They are afraid that if they grant this point of contact, they will surrender the uniqueness of biblical revelation.

I believe this fear is exaggerated. If man is made in the image of God (as Scripture says he is), then conservatives ought to welcome any evidence which helps establish a vital connection between the healing power of the gospel and man as a creature who is plagued by anxiety and estrangement. A divorce between common and special grace is an offense to both culture and the gospel.

In our enthusiasm to build on a point of contact, of course, we may inadvertently absorb the gospel into elements of a world system; for we do not know precisely where common grace leaves off and special grace begins. But if we are to get on with our vocation as Christians, we must accept this risk. Truth is advanced by open dialogue, not by silence.

In developing love as a point of contact between the gospel

and culture, I have appealed to the manners of a happy child. In so doing, however, I have constructed a chain of arguments that may strike critics as being either odd or trivial. But before my arguments are dismissed, let the critics make a serious effort to discover just what Jesus *did* mean when he said that we should humble ourselves and become like a child. It is possible that we are too sophisticated to perceive the relationship between the kingdom of heaven and the beautiful world of childhood.

In any event, I hope that my exploratory effort will encourage others to do a still better job. I believe that if Christian apologists would rally their wits and make better use of love as a point of contact, great things might be accomplished for the defense of the faith.

In an effort to please as well as instruct, I have based my remarks on a familiar story in the Bible. This story is found in the eleventh chapter of John. I have not been bound by the details of the story, nor have I allowed myself to wander into the wastelands of speculation.

The story can be recited by any Sunday school scholar: how Lazarus, a friend of Jesus, became ill; how Martha and Mary, the sisters of Lazarus, sent for Jesus; how Lazarus died before Jesus arrived; how Martha was offended when Jesus asked that the grave be unsealed; and how Jesus restored Lazarus to life.

I am writing from the viewpoint of Protestant orthodoxy. My goal is to show how the gospel can further man's search for a happy, integrated life. I do not say I have reached this goal; I only say I have tried. "It may be proper for all to remember, that they ought not to raise expectation which it is not in their power to satisfy, and that it is more pleasing to see smoke brightening into flame, than flame sinking into smoke."[4]

— E. J. C.

Fuller Theological Seminary
Pasadena, California

[4]Samuel Johnson, *The Rambler*, No. 1.

Contents

11

CHAPTER ONE

The Kingdom of Love

"Backward, turn backward, O Time, in your flight,
Make me a child again just for tonight!"
— Elizabeth Akers Allen

The Apostle John begins his story on a sad note. "Now a certain man was ill, Lazarus of Bethany, the village of Mary and her sister Martha" (John 11:1). We do not know what was wrong with Lazarus, but we soon learn that he was ill unto death.

A pious heart is disturbed by this. Lazarus trusted God. And from all we can discover, he was in the perfect will of God. Still, he was ill unto death. What about the people in Bethany who did not trust God, and yet went right on living? Was it fair that Lazarus should suffer and die?

I

Illness is an evil because it saps our strength. It leaves us damaged, like a wormy apple or a chipped vase. When we are ill, we are not the self we wish to be. We cannot do the things we want, and there is so much we really want to do.

If we are not too ill, there is one thing we *can* do, of course. We can let our minds wander. We can pretend that we are out in the fields finding hidden treasure or that we are soaring through distant, exciting lands. These are nice things to think about.

But there are some things that are not so nice, like death, for example. When we become ill, some part of our body is failing us; and when an important part fails, we die, that is all. Even a headache is advance warning that death is on the way. "It may be said that disease generally begins that equality which death completes; the distinctions which set one man so much above another are very little perceived in the gloom of a sick chamber, where it will be vain to expect entertainment from the gay, or instruction from the wise; where all human glory is obliterated, the wit is clouded, the reason perplexed, and the hero subdued; where the highest and brightest of mortal beings finds nothing left him but the consciousness of innocence."[1]

We may delay death by prudence and circumspection. But we cannot keep death from reaching us in the end. Death's knock may be gentle at first, very deceiving, as of a friend who awaits us. But soon the knock will become rude and insistent. Then we shall have to open the door, whether by day or by night.

If death follows a good plan, we do not know what that plan is, for all men die, whether young or old, good or bad. Death is like an immense tidal wave. Every hundred years or so it sweeps across the face of the earth, destroying everything in its path.

Some people are so afraid of death that they will not even talk about the grave. They do not avoid dying, but they think they have a better time living. They might have an even better time if they drew their wits about them and faced up to the limits which God has placed on the creation.

Some people despair. They are so weary of living that they

[1]Samuel Johnson, *The Rambler*, No. 48.

kill themselves. A few of these people have sick minds, but most of them simply lose hope. Unless we have faith in the future, we are doomed.

Some people view death as nothing but a part of nature's grand cycle. Nature is artistic, so they say. It creates while it destroys. Every leaf must fall to the forest floor, there to be gathered up again in the form of new life. This suggests that death is as natural as birth; we should submit to it with a sense of peaceful resignation.

But a pious person refuses to believe that death can be made lovely through poetry and song. Death is the king of terrors, for it separates us from our loved ones. When we lose love, we lose everything. Happy children know this, and so do all who remain children in heart.

II

The fear of death draws many people near to God. As they sense their own weakness, they long for resources that only God can give. By surrendering themselves to God, they believe that things will work out happily in the end. God will not forsake his friends.

But the fear of death also separates many from God. They are disturbed by the problem of evil. "If God is all-good and all-powerful," they want to know, "why did he create a world that arouses hope and then heartlessly crushes it?" A visit to the children's ward of a city hospital will show how serious the problem is. The children are filled with fear; they want to go home where they can be loved and cared for. But many of them will never go home. They will be taken from the hospital to the grave.

"It is so soon that I am done for, I wonder what I was begun for." This is an epitaph written for a dead infant. But it also sums up the sense of wonder that throbs in the heart of every man. Death may come today or tomorrow, but it is always an unwelcome visitor.

The amount of sorrow in the world passes human comprehension. The hospitals are always full, always understaffed. Even pious seekers after God have concluded that the present world is a scene of perpetual sorrow. "This," said Samuel Johnson in the last year of his life, "is my history; like all other histories, a narrative of misery."[2]

III

There is much evil in the world, yet everything is not evil. The setting sun, the wings of a butterfly, and the song of the wind — these are good, and the heart knows it.

Above all, there is love. Love is good because it communicates happy assurances that we are wanted and needed. We are born with an urge to count, and love gratifies this urge. The more we experience the joys of love, the more pleasant life becomes; and the more pleasant life becomes, the more we see just how good the world really is.

Happy children bear witness to the release that love brings. Though they may suffer a great deal, they do not despair, for love dissolves fear. As long as the children feel needed and wanted, they can endure everything else in hope.

Since children are too weak to go it alone, they are ready to trust others. This is the key to their security. Humility prepares the way for trust, and trust prepares the way for hope. Happy children are not afraid, for they know that their loved ones are watching over them.

Happy children are so full of love that they extend overtures of fellowship in every direction. They talk to their toys, they sing to their pets. The whole world is a kingdom of love. The days are too short to take in all the good things, the nights too long. Sleep is a thief and a robber, for it keeps the children from enjoying life to the full.

Since hope forms the very atmosphere of the kingdom of love, happy children have faith in the future. Faith is a sister of hope and love. Hope assures the heart that the conditions of

[2]Boswell, *Life of Johnson*, Britannica Great Books ed., Vol. 44, p. 561. Used by permission.

love will not be destroyed, not even by death itself. Faith rests in this assurance. Children may be very ill, but as long as they abide in the kingdom of love they go right on believing that things will work out happily in the end.

Since love and hope go together, children improve the foundations of hope by improving the foundations of love. They extend a warm welcome to friends everywhere. When Santa Claus visits a hospital, the children sit tall with excitement. They forget their sorrows, for the very air is charged with a spirit of good will.

Hope brings joy. As long as children feel needed and wanted, they are happy citizens in the kingdom of love. Love waves its magic wand and an open field becomes an enchanted forest. Tall castles and dancing elves can be seen in the distance. Children not only give names to rabbits and squirrels, but they count the trees among their very best friends.

IV

Since happy children are citizens of the kingdom of love, they enjoy an intuitive perception of virtue. When adults are asked to tell what virtue is, they often give the impression that the task is beyond their capacity. Haven't the greatest philosophers failed to agree on a definition? How, then, can common people succeed?

If happy children were to hear of this, they might be somewhat amused, for they discover the meaning of virtue by listening to their own hearts. Whether the intellect will own it or not, the heart has its convictions. *These convictions say that a person is good when he is kind and truthful, and that in the end a good person has nothing to fear.* The first part clarifies love, while the second part clarifies hope. To love is to be kind and truthful; to hope is to believe that things will work out happily in the end. The issue is as simple as that.

Some may complain that the convictions of the heart are only a figment of the imagination. If children have such convictions, so the complaint goes, why don't they spell them out for others to see?

The answer is, children *do* spell out these convictions, though they do it in a form that can only be seen by those who are children in heart. Happy children project their convictions in the form of stories or fairy tales. These stories are built about a dramatic conflict between good and evil. Children can enter into this conflict because they are already familiar with the virtues that form the kingdom of love.

For example, Little Black Sambo is good because he wants to be a friend of the tigers. But the tigers are bad. They refuse to honor the boy's trust. So, happy children say that Little Black Sambo has a perfect right to eat a stack of pancakes topped with butter made from the selfish tigers.

As long as children feel needed and wanted, they have no difficulty judging the conflict between good and evil in a fairy tale, and thus the conflict in life itself. Culture may change the scenery, but the conflict remains the same. Do good people count, or do they not? This is the issue. The heart says they do, and happy children rest in the verdict of the heart. The conflict between good and evil can take place in a fairy tale, in imagination, or in real life. The setting makes no difference.

Since one language is spoken in the kingdom of love, there is no confusion of tongues. This means that if all the happy children in the world could be gathered together, they would enjoy the story of Cinderella. They would be drawn by convictions that originate deep in the heart. Cinderella is kind and gentle; she does what she is told; and she helps the weak. Since she is a good girl, she is entitled to live happily ever after. If Cinderella were to be overwhelmed by evil, not only would the kingdom of love be destroyed, but children would be stripped of their native assurance that good people have nothing to fear. The scheming stepmother may *seem* to be winning out, but the heart compels children to believe that things will change. And sure enough, a fairy godmother appears and Cinderella goes to the royal ball. "See," the children say, "I *told* you so!" Since they were held by the convictions of the heart, they knew all along that something like this would happen. It would only be a matter of time.

V

Although parents enjoy reading fairy tales to their children, they seldom see any connection between the logic of these tales and the logic of life itself. They think they are only entertaining their children, when in truth they are performing a work of love. They are assuring their children that the convictions of the heart *are* trustworthy.

The fairy tales are an image of general history, seen through the eyes of a child. A bad ending to these tales would threaten the values that the child already takes for granted. There may be a great deal of evil in life, just as there is in a fairy tale, but the evil is not so great that the conditions of love are dissolved. Take away love, and what is left? Children know the answer, and so do all who remain children in heart. If love is lost, all is lost. This is why the outcome of a fairy tale is a very serious matter.

Adults may scoff at the intuitive powers of a child, but there was one man who did not, and that was Jesus Christ. In fact, Jesus was so mindful of a child's wisdom that he advised his disciples to heed this wisdom in their own lives. "And calling to him a child, he put him in the midst of them, and said, 'Truly, I say to you, unless you turn and become like children, you will never enter the kingdom of heaven. Whoever humbles himself like this child, he is the greatest in the kingdom of heaven'" (Matthew 18:2-4). Since happy children belong to the kingdom of love, they are already familiar with the virtues that make up the kingdom of heaven; for the kingdom of heaven is the eternal phase of the kingdom of love.

Happy children complete their lives through love; they are not deceived into thinking that security can be gained by power and influence. Children often quarrel, of course, thus testifying to their imperfection. But at the end of the day, when the real

19

ground for living is sought, happy children rest in securities that only love can bring.

When we become like a child, we do not surrender the responsibilities of adulthood, nor do we become uncritical in judgment. Rather, we consciously take up residence in the kingdom of love. And we do this by resisting the temptation to think that we can complete our lives without accepting the duties of love. These duties are plain to all who wait on the Holy Spirit. To love is to be kind and truthful.

A child may be very weak; he may have little power and few possessions. But these shortcomings need not disturb him. As long as the child feels needed and wanted, he is too content with what he has to worry about what he lacks. Being loved in the present, he is not afraid of the future. He can yield himself to life with a sense of complete abandon.

Adults are just as helpless as children, for illness and death show no respect of persons. But adults have just enough strength to be deceived into thinking that they can defy the limits that God has set on the creation. They imagine that they can save themselves through power.

VI

Many people admit that it would be *nice* to rest in the convictions of the heart, and thus to enjoy hope. But they say they honestly have no idea what these convictions are. The heart is laced with many conflicting feelings. How can any one feeling be elevated above another?

If happy children could express themselves, they would say that such people are either not looking in the right place, or they do not have the eyes of their understanding opened by the Holy Spirit.

For example, our heart tells us how to act when we visit a sick child. We know that unless we show signs of love, we wound the child and degrade ourselves. The child is weak and lonely; he craves fresh assurances that his life counts. Love is charged with responsibility to communicate these assurances.

We must bring the child a gift, hold his hand, and by every word and gesture assure him that things are just fine in the kingdom of love.

This should not be too difficult to accept, for if we were in the place of the child, we would want our own hope strengthened; and we would want it strengthened by people who tell the truth. A good man does as he would be done by. This is the first duty of love. Thus, if we assure a child that all is well in the kingdom of love, when in fact we are not even citizens of this kingdom, we are guilty of the worst sort of deception. Hope must rest on reality, not fiction.

The heart also tells us how to act when we attend a funeral. A good person knows that he is commissioned with the task of strengthening hope. This ministry is never more welcome than when death has rendered its melancholy verdict. Since the bereaved have united their hearts with the departed, they cannot believe that death has spoken the last word. They know that if the dead do not count, then the living do not count, for the living and the dead form one unbroken fellowship. Thus, a good person will do his best to assure the bereaved that death has not dissolved the kingdom of love, and that in the kingdom of heaven there will be a renewal of lost fellowship. This means that whenever a person communicates assurances of hope to the bereaved, he is really saying that the soul is immortal and that God will overrule the verdict of death.

Once we humble ourselves and become like a child, we discover that the convictions of the heart are active whenever our own security is seriously threatened. If our health is taken away, if we fear the imminence of death, or if we lose our freedom or our rights, power and pretense become empty and we are once again cast on the simplicities of the kingdom of love. For example, prisoners of war sustain hope by devising new ways to be of service to one another. As long as they have a reason for existence, hope stays alive; and this reason is created by works of love. Again, psychologists find that some patients suffer from no clinically definable neurosis. Instead, they suffer from a feeling of senselessness and emptiness that drains life of hope. Only works of love can dissipate this feeling.

The convictions of the heart are also active when we grow old and our strength ebbs away. Elderly people have run life's course; they have experienced the futility of personal striving; they realize that love is the only thing that matters. As long as they feel needed and wanted, they can bear all else in patience.

VII

"But if the convictions of the heart are so near at hand," some may inquire, "why do they play such a minor role in the real business of life?" The answer is, the convictions of the heart play a *major* role, but for certain reasons this role is hindered from entering the conscious life, and thus from being acknowledged by the intellect.

One reason for this interference is that adults must earn their daily bread in a competitive society that leaves little time for reflection on spiritual things. While children are free to romp in the kingdom of love, adults must assemble automobiles in a plant that may close from lack of supplies or a drop in business. The resulting anxiety may be so great that the convictions of the heart, however active, do not come to the attention of consciousness.

But this is not the profound reason why the convictions of the heart seem to play such a minor role in the real business of life. Jesus says that any normal person can prepare for the kingdom of heaven by becoming like a child. Our difficulty is that we fail to make this preparation. Pride draws us away from the kingdom of love, and thus from the kingdom of heaven, by tempting us to think that we can dispense with the duties of love. We do not share our lives with others, nor do we make it easy for others to share their lives with us. We prefer to remain unattached. When we deceive ourselves long enough, hardness of heart sets in; and this hardness, in turn, blinds us to the seriousness of our loss.

We may go right on living, of course, but our reason for

living will not endure scrutiny. *Valid* hope looks to a social order in which the conditions of love will survive the shock of death, and only God has power to create such an order.

Pride wants the benefits of hope, though it rejects the duties of love. But this will not do, for the kingdom of heaven completes and fulfills the kingdom of love. This is why Jesus appealed to the humility of a child. "Then children were brought to him that he might lay his hands on them and pray. The disciples rebuked the people; but Jesus said, 'Let the children come to me, and do not hinder them; for to such belongs the kingdom of heaven'" (Matthew 19:13-14). Whoever would enter the kingdom of heaven must first enter the kingdom of love.

CHAPTER TWO

The Limits of Science

"If at some period in the course of civilization we seriously find that our science and our religion are antagonistic, then there must be something wrong either with our science or with our religion."

— Havelock Ellis

After Martha and Mary had done all they could to help their ailing brother, they sent for Jesus. "So the sisters sent to him, saying, 'Lord, he whom you love is ill'" (John 11:3). Martha and Mary were ready to trust Jesus with all their heart, for he not only was a man sent from God, but he embodied every virtue set down by the convictions of the heart. His actions were kind, his words were truthful. Jesus was the number-one citizen in the kingdom of love. Children came to him gladly, and so did all who were children in heart.

I

The faith of Martha and Mary seems strangely out of place in an age of science. In our zeal to interpret and control nature, we have lost sight of the kingdom of love, and thus of the kingdom of heaven. We are afraid to dream; we are critical of religious symbolism; and we live in the thin world of statistics. We have alienated ourselves from the ground of our being by divesting the universe of its sense of mystery. Natural law has displaced divine providence. And with mystery goes joy. The trees no longer clap their hands, the little hills no longer leap like lambs. The sense of awe that once hovered over the priest now hovers over the scientist.

The achievements of science are great, to be sure. When we walk through the halls of an institute of technology, we face such a complex of instruments that the convictions of the heart, and thus the connections between hope and love, seem vague and unconvincing. How can the convictions of the heart stand up to the precision of an electronic computer? When tested by the scientific method, these convictions have no more claim to reality than leprechauns or fictional pots of gold.

Since we are all debtors to science (even the lamp on our desk is a fruit of technology), little would be gained, and much lost, by thinking that we can return to the simple ways of Martha and Mary. Time brings changes, and these changes must be accepted as part of the dramatic element in history.

When Jesus told his disciples to imitate the manners of a child, he did not expect them to forfeit the pleasure of interpreting and controlling nature. He did, however, warn them against the temptation of becoming so absorbed with the signs of the *sky* that they overlooked the signs of the *times*. Man is spirit as well as body.

Happy children are full of questions. They want to know all about nature. Why are trees green? What keeps the sun in place? How does a bird know where to build its nest? The seeds of scientific curiosity were planted in the heart by God himself.

Moreover, when children ask questions, they are trying to relieve their fear of not counting. Knowledge brings power, and power brings security. Ignorance is such a cruel taskmaster that only a want of either ability or resolution keeps a person from knowing all that can be known. Samuel Johnson perceived this with rare insight. "All knowledge is of itself of some value.

25

There is nothing so minute or inconsiderable, that I would not rather know it than not. In the same manner, all power, of whatever sort, is of itself desirable. A man would not submit to learn to hem a ruffle, of his wife, or his wife's maid; but if a mere wish could attain it, he would rather wish to be able to hem a ruffle."[1]

But interpreting and controlling nature is more than a pleasure. It is a solemn duty, for the very safety of our lives may be at stake. Children know this, and so do all who remain children in heart. If Cinderella were deliberately to stand beneath a falling tree, she would elicit no pity from children. Whoever presumes upon nature must live with the consequences of his choice. Thus, when a mariner puts to sea, he must study the weather and the tides. Otherwise, he has no right to expect a safe voyage.

From this it would appear that the scientific method is simply common sense become technical. A prudent housewife does not hang out her laundry until she checks to see if it is going to rain. A meteorologist adds precision to this effort because he has more accurate measuring instruments. A navigator bases his calculations on the conclusions of science, not on the opinions of a housewife.

Therefore, if a zealot were to attack the scientific method in the name of religion, he would only announce what a dreadful religion he has. The urge to interpret and control nature belongs to the image of God in man. When Adam was placed in the Garden of Eden, he was given something to do. He was to tend the Garden and rule over the animal kingdom. He was told, as it were, to be a good scientist; for how could he subdue nature unless he developed techniques by which nature is subdued?

II

If Jesus were to address a scientific faculty, he might disarm his auditors by his warm words of commendation. But he would

[1]Boswell, *Life of Johnson,* Britannica Great Books ed., Vol. 44, p. 256. Used by permission.

not end the matter there. Scientists are human beings, and as human beings they must come to terms with the kingdom of love. Otherwise, they may make the mistake of thinking that they can complete their lives through science. A happy child welcomes the power that knowledge brings, but in the end he rests his hope in love, not power. He that is wise, says Jesus, will go and do likewise. "For what does it profit a man, to gain the whole world and forfeit his life? For what can a man give in return for his life?" (Mark 8:36-37). Science has no cure for senility and death.

If Jesus were to defend the ground of hope, he might advise scientists to examine the ties that bind the fraternity of science itself. These ties are actually woven from the convictions of the heart. Degrees of good and evil in the fraternity of science, no less than in the kingdom of love, are measured by kindness and truth. Every upright scientist knows that it is wrong to use another man's research without his permission. The scientist judges the issue with the same intuitive skill with which a child judges the dramatic conflict between good and evil in a fairy tale. To cheat another person is *wrong*, that is all there is to it. Both the scientist and the child are governed by standards that are neither discovered nor defended by the scientific method.

When the scientist leaves the laboratory and goes about daily life, he judges his fellow man in precisely the same way that he judges his fellow scientist. He will call no man good who is unkind and untruthful. On the highway, in the market, or around the hearth, he expects others to treat him as a human being. If his dignity is outraged or his rights are defrauded, he instinctively judges the offending party guilty; and he keeps right on judging until he either forgets the incident or the offending party sets things right.

One conclusion is unavoidable. When a scientist passes judgment on evil people, he not only bears witness to the convictions of the heart, but he announces the limits of science. Since moral judgments are in the imperative mood (they tell what *ought*

27

to be), while scientific judgments are in the descriptive mood (they tell what *is*), there is no way that moral judgments can be either affirmed or denied by the scientific method.

What, then, is the problem? The problem is that modern man tends to invest the scientific method with more authority than it deserves. As a result, a premium is put on intellectual detachment. We lose sight of the kingdom of love, and thus of the kingdom of heaven, in our very zeal to interpret and control nature. Intellectual detachment has no way of knowing what goes on in either kingdom.

This is why Jesus says we must humble ourselves and become like a child. If Jesus' disciples were deceived in an age of faith, have we any reason to think that we shall not be deceived in an age of science? Unless we keep in tune with the convictions of the heart, we may be deluded into thinking that we can enjoy the benefits of hope without submitting to the duties of love.

The delusion begins whenever we say that the convictions of the heart do not rank as knowledge, and thus are inferior in authority to the principles of science. The plain truth is that these convictions command attention long before, and long after, an interest in the scientific method is aroused. A student would never become a chemist or a physicist unless he were persuaded that his colleagues were trustworthy. Deception is evil, whether in the fraternity of science or out of it; and it is evil because it is a direct offspring of selfishness. A selfish person is not kind and truthful; he refuses to do as he would be done by.

A scientist may approach the world of nature with intellectual detachment. But when he approaches issues involving values and morals, he must judge as man and not as scientist. And to do this, the heart must join forces with the mind.

III

By admitting the convictions of the heart into the rank of knowledge, we in no way prejudice the rights of science, nor do we open the sluice gate for superstition; for what *is* the mark of good procedure, if not an unswerving devotion to actual experience?

When we have a fixed standard of goodness, we know what to think of a demagogue who outrages our dignity or defrauds our rights. We judge him evil, and we use every legitimate weapon to impede his nefarious schemes. A decent society is regulated by the axiom that a man is good when he is kind and truthful. The fact that this axiom flows from the convictions of the heart, and not from the scientific method, is no mark in its disfavor. The moment we become sophisticated about the convictions of the heart, we give aid and comfort to those who view human beings as mere digits, and who thus feel no moral responsibility to defend the dignity and rights of the individual. We need only remember the manner in which the German universities prepared the way for Hitler.[2] The universities could not sound a clear moral note because such an outcry would have been "unscientific." Human beings were used for medical experiments, while the ashes of the cremated were used for fertilizer. The triumph of intellectual detachment prepared Germany for the second world war.

Since scientists are human beings as well as scientists, they would do society a singular service if (as human beings) they announced, and kept on announcing, that intellectual detachment is invalid when judgments about morals and values are made. And in the real business of daily life, we make these judgments all the time.

For example, the threat of atomic war now hangs over us. The prospect of total destruction shocks the very scientists who developed the weapons of destruction.[3] And why are they shocked? They are shocked because they are moved by the convictions of the heart, the same convictions that move a child when the wicked witch tries to put Hansel and Gretel into the oven. Whenever evil becomes a threat to the self — either in fact or by way of dramatic identification — the heart cannot be

[2]See Frederic Lilge, *The Abuse of Learning* (Macmillan).
[3]See Robert Jungk, *Brighter Than a Thousand Suns* (Harcourt, Brace).

neutral. The very being of the self is involved; the threat is no longer academic. And it makes little difference whether the threat is expressed in a malicious remark, an unprovoked blow, or atomic war. The spiritual dignity of the self is the base from which all spontaneous moral judgments are made.

If a scientist were to return home and find a hoodlum terrorizing his wife and children, he would not judge with intellectual detachment. He would take decisive action to overpower the hoodlum, for the convictions of the heart would join forces with the claims of the mind.

But it is not enough for scientists to *know* that detachment is out of bounds when values and morals are judged. As human beings they must stand up and *say* they know this. The world is locked in a great moral struggle. Unless we recover a crusading zeal for righteousness, we may lose both the fraternity of science and our way of life.

Jesus says that we should humble ourselves and become like a child. A child, let us remember, is not afraid to express himself. He knows who is good and who is evil, and he is forthright in saying so.

When we allow ourselves to fall into habits of detachment, we lose the feelings of moral certitude that come from the convictions of the heart. As a result, we hesitate to commit ourselves on the critical issues of the day. We realize that the cynical elements in communism are evil. But we do precious little about translating this into a working philosophy of history. By surrendering our feelings of moral certitude, we hand the initiative to communism.

IV

Science has justly earned its reputation as a precise method for interpreting and controlling nature. Nonetheless, we must remind ourselves that science deals with aspects of reality that are less accessible, and thus less certain, than those that a child judges when he is held by the convictions of the heart. Science tries to discover the laws that lie behind the elemental particles in the universe; but it cannot make a final formulation of these laws, for it lacks immediate access to the elemental particles. It can only infer the nature of such particles by their gross effects in the universe.

By way of contrast, the heart *has* immediate access to the elemental particles of virtue. Every happy child knows that a man is good when he is kind and truthful, and so does every person who is a child at heart.

Science can get no closer to the elemental particles of the universe than the thresholds of sensation will permit. This is why the history of science is a history of displaced hypotheses. There can be no final scientific truth, for the elemental particles will always be just out of reach. Neither our human faculties nor our scientific instruments can go above the upper threshold of sensation, or descend beneath the lower. For example, if we cut a piece of string into smaller and smaller pieces, eventually we reach the place where we no longer have any string. And what is more disturbing, we can never be perfectly sure what we have in its place.

Science lengthens the diameter of knowledge, but at the same time it widens the circumference of ignorance. Scientific judgments will remain tentative for the last man on earth; for the last man, no less than the first, will be denied immediate access to the elemental particles of the universe.

Since the heart is not hindered by the thresholds of sensation, moral judgments are subject to less revision than scientific judgments. The Sermon on the Mount is as relevant today as it was when Jesus first preached it. Jesus dealt with issues of beatitude (happiness), and these issues draw on the convictions of the heart. A man is blessed when he honors the duties that make up the kingdom of love. Such a man, like happy children about him, is a fit subject for the kingdom of heaven.

From time to time it is asserted that the day is not far off when even the thoughts of man will be subject to scientific control. Such dreadful prophecies reveal the extent to which detachment can remain oblivious to things that are native to the heart of a child. Human beings are partly in nature, and to this degree are subject to scientific manipulation. But in the center of their person they enjoy freedom over nature. This freedom is the spring of creativity in the scientific method itself. A student dedicates himself to science because he is freely attracted to the discipline, not because he is acting out of natural necessity. Nature has its principle of motion and rest in itself (Aristotle), while freedom implies an unfettered response to values and morals. A freely inspired person does what he wants to because he wants to. For example, a scientist arranges his desk to suit himself. He will not justify his arrangement by a logic higher than his own preferences, and he is offended if he is asked to do so. He refuses to be treated as a thing.

When intellectual detachment classifies human beings as nothing but aspects of nature, it illustrates the depravity of human nature as well as the presumed moral neutrality under which this depravity takes shelter. No child could be persuaded that baby brother is only a complex of the same chemical and physical forces that make up a rat. Baby brother can love, and no rat can do that. Love is the highest and finest fruit of human freedom, and its duties are first introduced into consciousness through the convictions of the heart.

Many scientists are willing to take a responsible part in man's present struggle for survival, but all too often they enlist only as scientists, not as human beings. Rather than drawing on the convictions of the heart, and thus giving depth to their judgments, they propose that we solve our impasse by a "crash program" which draws on the full resources of the scientific method. By making such a proposal, however, they prove that they neither grasp the issues at stake nor have they any special insights to solve them.

<h2 style="text-align:center">V</h2>

On at least one occasion Jesus likened himself to a physician. This is very instructive, for it suggests what is possibly the most telling reason why a conflict between science and the convictions of the heart is neither desirable nor necessary.

A physician is committed to a unique vocation. He cannot

get on with it as scientist until he accepts responsibilities that connect with the convictions of the heart. Scientific competence is not enough. The physician must create a spiritual bond between the patient and himself. He must ask, "How are you today? Now, sit down and tell me about your difficulty." And when he shows an interest, he must really mean it. To *pretend* to be interested will not do.

The physician must be both scientist and human being at the same time. He must view his patient as a part of nature, yet not altogether so. He brings healing as a scientist, yet he cannot storm his patient with the scientific method. If his patient suspects that he is being treated as a thing, and not as a person, he will quickly find another physician.

A physician is given access to the concealed parts of the body. Everything is revealed, nothing is hidden. But no normal person will disrobe unless he is convinced that his physician is a trustworthy person.

In an effort to keep unscrupulous individuals out of the medical profession, a physician enters his office under the terms of a solemn oath. "I swear by Apollo the physician, and Aesculapius, and Health, and All-heal, and all the gods and goddesses, that, according to my ability and judgment, I will keep this Oath. . . . I will follow that system of regimen which, according to my ability and judgment, I consider for the benefit of my patients, and abstain from whatever is deleterious and mischievous. I will give no deadly medicine to any one if asked, nor suggest any such counsel. . . . With purity and with holiness I will pass my life and practice my Art. . . . Into whatever houses I enter, I will go into them for the benefit of the sick, and will abstain from every voluntary act of mischief and corruption; and, further from the seduction of females or males, of freemen and slaves. Whatever, in connection with my professional practice, or not in connection with it, I see or hear, in the life of men, which ought not to be spoken of abroad, I will not divulge, as reckoning that all such should be kept secret. . . ." The Hippocratic Oath is a remarkable professional code. While it has some dated elements, its substance contains timeless moral truths. Hippocrates managed this by subordinating the claims of science to the convictions of the heart. Unless a physician is a good man, he has no right to call himself a physician; and he is not a good man unless he is kind and truthful. Good men, whether in medicine or out of it, do as they would be done by.

This means that physicians swear by insights that are more ultimate than those of science. A physician must surround his practice with gentle proofs that his patients are human beings. He must never betray confidence; he must be discreet at all times.

When scientists become ill, they likewise send for a physician. But they will not reveal their secrets unless they are convinced that the physician is an upright individual. One important conclusion follows. Since scientists are able to pass judgment upon the moral qualifications of a physician, they surely would not advance the cause of truth if they insisted that *all* knowledge is subject to the scientific method. They know that a bad person cannot be a good physician, and they know it by the convictions of the heart, not by the scientific method. And since they know this, they ought to *announce* that they know it; though they must announce it as human beings, not as scientists.

VI

When a physician heals the sick, he is dedicated to a task that is defeated from its inception. The patient seeks convincing signs that his life counts, and the physician does his best to give these signs. But the physician acts under the shadow of an untruth, for the patient actually has *much* to fear. Science teaches (according to the Second Law of Thermodynamics) that the energy in the universe, though constant, is tending to neutralize. If enough time lapses, all life will perish, for energy will no longer be available for work. Now, if death is to win in the end, how can a patient have hope?

Nor is this all. Even though a physician has access to many case histories, this access gives him no advantage when the logic of suffering is explored. To what moral law can he, as scientist, appeal? There is no evidence of distributive justice in the wards of a hospital. A virtuous man is often put to the rack, while a corrupt man walks free.

The physician's silence about the logic of suffering should be noted with care, for it shows that the scientific method is not qualified to make Messianic promises. If the physician succeeds in communicating hope to his patient, he succeeds because he is a citizen in the kingdom of love, not because he has penetrated the mystery of existence by the scientific method.

VII

When Martha and Mary sent for Jesus, they acted from the same interests that prompt us to send for a physician. Jesus was kind in his manners, truthful in his words. And he knew his office well, for the very creative energy of God flowed through him. He not only diagnosed the exact nature of every disease, but he often effected cures by the mere word of his mouth.

A physician is neither as virtuous nor as powerful as Jesus. He is kind and truthful some of the time, but not all of the time. And his control over disease is never absolute, for the laws of medicine break down when they touch the mystery of individual life. For example, a highly nervous patient can show symptoms which resemble those of an organic disease. A patient can become totally blind, though possessing two perfectly normal eyes. He can suffer deafness, paralysis of an arm, loss of speech, or even experience symptoms of pregnancy. A physician must be content with fractional truths. When he heals, he must credit some of his success to fortune.

Still, a physician is living proof that the convictions of the heart and the scientific method can be blended in one dignified vocation. If we examine this proof with the care that it deserves, we may find that we are already dealing with a body of evidences that point to the person of Jesus Christ.

CHAPTER THREE

The Limits of Philosophy

"We are born to inquire after truth."

— Montaigne

When Martha and Mary sent for Jesus, they knew how desperate the situation was. Their brother's life hung in the balance; everything turned on the timely arrival of Jesus. Yet, the sisters did not come right out and ask Jesus to make haste, nor did they dwell on their desperation. Or, at least it does not *appear* that they did, for all they said was, "Lord, he whom you love is ill" (John 11:3).

In any case, Martha and Mary were forthright as children. They had something to say, and they came right out and said it. Friends enjoy a holy boldness that would offend the ceremonies of the world. Love has open manners. It conceals nothing, for it fears nothing. "There is no fear in love, but perfect love casts out fear. For fear has to do with punishment, and he who fears is not perfected in love" (I John 4:18).

Martha and Mary took things just as they were. They were not clever or sophisticated. Lazarus was ill, and that was all there was to it. No metaphysical subtleties could persuade the sisters that illness was only an error of the material sense.

The sisters were childlike in their approach to reality. A child opens his heart, and in rushes the world with all its captivating freshness. His words are rich with meaning because they are rich with experience. If you ask him what he means by "cat," he will take you to the corner of the room where Tabby is sleeping. "See that?" he will ask. "Well, *that's* what I mean by cat!"

A child loves familiar ways. He wants a world that he can depend on. And in order to have these things, he accepts life as it is. He does not try to make things over to suit his tastes or his mind. If experience tells him that rocks are hard, then rocks are hard, that is all there is to it. Nothing more can be said on the subject — nothing fruitful, that is.

I

Once we leave the wonderful world of childhood, we can never again return. Our faculties have awakened; the artless manners of a child will no longer do. A child can see a bridge, but he cannot see the laws of engineering that go into a bridge.

With intellectual awakening comes a thrill unknown to childhood, for a disciplined mind can raise questions about the ultimate meaning of life. Behold Socrates standing in the fields, gazing into the heavens as he meditates on where man has come from, what he is doing here, and where he is going. Just to watch him is an inspiration.

But intellectual awakening has perils, for the mind can play tricks on us — and just when we think it is most dependable. It promises to lead us closer to reality, while all the while it takes us farther away. For example, some philosophers have argued that *everything* is in motion, while others, with equal force, have argued that *nothing* is in motion. And the curious part of such arguments is that they were devised in all seriousness. Now, if a child were to hear of this, he would wonder how intelligent people could drift so far from things as they are.

By staying next to reality, he would know that some things are in motion, while other things are not. Rivers change, but the convictions of the heart remain the same.

Why do philosophers doubt things that are self-evident? The answer is, they limit reality to what they can *conceive,* rather than to what they *experience.* This is a perilous procedure, for if we are to get on with our task of interpreting reality, we must acknowledge that many things are inconceivable. Sleep is a mystery. The conception and formation of a child transcend explanation. We do not know what life is, even though we ourselves are living creatures. But our failure to conceive these things is certainly no reason to deny them. We should submit to reality, not try to make it over. If we find that it is raining outside, we should not argue that the weather is dry.

Since philosophers will only believe what they can conceive, they are more prey to speculation than scientists are. Nature is a check against the claims of science, but not against the claims of philosophy. This is one reason why the history of philosophy is more erratic than the history of science.

Unless we stay close to reality itself, we shall separate ourselves from the kingdom of love, and thus from the kingdom of heaven. Rather than deriving feelings of moral certitude from the convictions of the heart, we shall dwell in the gray world of concepts.

When Samuel Johnson kicked a tree to answer Berkeley's contention that nothing but ideas exist, he was really telling Berkeley to get back to reality. A stubbed toe is convincing proof that there is more to life than ideas. A child knows this, and so do all who remain children in heart. When reason takes us away from things that are clearly presented in experience, it has failed in its office.

Let us remember the famous centipede who got along nicely until he was asked how he managed to walk. The awakening of reason proved to be his undoing, for the more he tried to account for the mechanics of locomotion, the more perplexed he became. In the end he lay down on the grass, quite unable to move. Since he could not conceive the *possibility* of walking, he was forced to deny its *reality*.

We find this amusing. But when human beings deny what they cannot conceive, the matter is no longer humorous. Intellectual detachment can call our most fundamental values into question.

II

Socrates illustrates the way in which philosophers fall into the predicament of the centipede. Socrates went from the fields to the market place, there to find a self-consistent definition of virtue. Now, since every happy child knows that a man is good when he is kind and truthful, surely Socrates, with his vast acumen and undaunted courage, should have had little difficulty knowing as much. But tradition tells us that he died a cautious skeptic. A lifetime of searching failed to bring him to certainties that children take for granted when they judge the conflict between good and evil in a fairy tale.

The problem is perfectly illustrated by Socrates' conversation with the young moralist, Euthyphro. When Socrates inquired about the nature of piety, Euthyphro had a ready answer. "Piety is doing as I am doing; that is to say, prosecuting any one who is guilty of murder, sacrilege, or of any similar crime — whether he be your father or mother, or whoever he may be, that makes no difference — and not to prosecute them is impiety." Socrates commended the youth, though he went on to add, "Remember that I did not ask you to give me two or three examples of piety, but to explain the general idea which makes all pious things to be pious." In due season Euthyphro argued that piety is doing the good, and that the good is what is loved by the gods; only to have Socrates remind him that the gods themselves are divided on the question.

Well, this was enough for Euthyphro, and off he went to court, there to prosecute his father for murder. Socrates sat on the Porch of King Archon, brooding over his failure. "Alas! my companion, and will you leave me in despair? I was hoping that you would instruct me in the nature of piety and impiety."[1]

If a child were to spend an afternoon with Socrates, he would be drawn by the charms of this great philosopher. The child would forthrightly say that Socrates was a virtuous man, for he was kind and truthful. And in saying this, he would say what Plato himself said. Plato was so moved by the example of Socrates that he dedicated his own life to the cause of philosophy. Now, if Socrates was kind and truthful, he must have known the nature of virtue, despite his seeming agnosticism. The convictions of the heart govern the groves of Academe as well as the fraternity of science; for whenever Socrates and his friends gathered to discuss the essence of virtue, they could not get on with it unless they embodied the very essence that they sought. There simply *is* no friendship apart from kindness and truth.

But if Socrates knew the meaning of virtue, why did he say he did not? The answer, it would seem, is that he knew it intuitively (in his heart, that is), though not in his intellect. He could not *conceive* the essence of virtue.

But it is to the eternal credit of Socrates that he did not deny what he could not conceive. He did not stop being kind and truthful because he could not formulate a self-consistent definition of virtue. He toyed with the idea that the real man is the rational man, and that man is at his best when he is thinking. But in his honest self he could not rest in such an idea. So, he preferred to remain a cautious skeptic.

III

Although Plato was moved by the Socratic standard of virtue, he did not make the best use of this standard, and neither did Aristotle. Both philosophers shifted from kindness and truth to a beatific vision of the world of Ideas. In other words, they limited virtue to what they could conceive.

[1] This sparkling discussion is found in the *Euthyphro,* 5b-16.

They did not realize that such a procedure was utterly at variance with the real business of living. A child knows the meaning of virtue by letting his heart speak, and so do all who humble themselves and become like a child. In real life a person is good when he is kind and truthful, not when he is skilled at rational dialectic. Brilliant people are often pompous egotists.

After Plato shifted from kindness and truth to rational dialectic, he was free to enlist the claims of philosophy in the service of pride. After all, wasn't Plato a skilled dialectician? Surely he must be virtuous.

Plato was not satisfied until he constructed a social order in which the philosopher was king. Only the philosopher could be entrusted with rule, for he alone was able to make contact with the world of Ideas through rational dialectic. And from this fountain of clear and distinct ideas would flow a stream of moral virtues needed to regulate society. Whoever sees the right will do the right. Thus, an ideal philosopher is noble, generous, the friend of truth, justice, courage, and temperance. "Then, besides other qualities, we must try to find a naturally well-proportioned and gracious mind, which will move spontaneously towards the true being of everything."[2] The philosopher is virtuous because he converses with the divine order. He thus becomes orderly and divine, as far as the nature of man allows.

Plato drew a straight line between the philosophers and the gods. And so did Aristotle. An ideal philosopher is most like the gods because his powers of rational dialectic deliver him from passion and prejudice. It did not occur to the Greeks that the intellect is often a willing servant of pride.

Whether we care to own it or not, arguments seem more logical when they support our interests. Plato was convinced that only a philosopher was fit to be a king. But if slaves, soldiers, and merchants were to draw up a Republic, they would argue that *they* were more virtuous, and thus more entitled to

---

[2]*Republic,* 486c.

rule than the philosophers. Their argument would seem logical because it would buttress personal interest. The slaves, soldiers, and merchants would imitate Plato in assuming that reason is innocent and impartial. They would overlook the manner in which we believe what we want to believe. Or as Pascal puts it, "The will is one of the chief factors in belief, not that it creates belief, but because things are true or false according to the aspect in which we look at them. The will, which prefers one aspect to another, turns away the mind from considering the qualities of all that it does not like to see; and thus the mind, moving in accord with the will, stops to consider the aspect which it likes, and so judges by what it sees."[3]

If little children were to hear how Plato treated a slave (a slave is "a troublesome piece of goods"), they might have difficulty going to sleep at night. Their hearts would speak louder than their intellects. They would pity a slave, for they would put themselves in his place. Love would constrain them to do as they would be done by, and *they* certainly would not want to be treated as a slave. Plato felt no pity because he took shelter in the chambers of intellectual detachment. Rational dialectic, not love, was the highest human virtue. And it was highest because it knows no probability. "Then dialectic, and dialectic alone, goes directly to the first principle and is the only science which does away with hypotheses in order to make her ground secure."[4] Since Plato found it logical to believe that a slave is inferior to a freeman, that ended the matter for him.

IV

Fortunately, Plato confined his Republic to hypothetical conditions. This is why we can examine his social philosophy with a measure of historical curiosity. But when intellectual detachment is entrusted with the real affairs of life, curiosity turns to dread.

[3]*Pensées,* 99.
[4]*Republic,* 553c.

We need only think of Alfred Rosenberg as an extreme but frightfully real example of what we mean. Rosenberg was the semi-official philosopher of the National Socialist Party, the party that brought Hitler to power. Using the concept of German autonomy as his major premise, he found it quite in accord with logic to argue that the German race is superior to other races. Nietzsche said that morality is nothing but a weapon for group power, and Rosenberg translated this into a defense of National Socialism. Whatever advances the Nazi cause is good; whatever hinders it is evil. There is not, and there could not be, such a tribunal as international law. Law is only an expedient to augment the power of the state. Force decides what is right.

Nazi tyranny illustrates what can happen when intellectual detachment is entrusted with the task of defining the real conditions in life. Pride imagines that its goals are the goals of the gods, and that will-to-power is an innocent attempt to bring time into conformity with eternity.

In our own day communism gratifies the resentments of those who seek the overthrow of capitalism, and who are anxious to invest their interests with the sanction of logic. This explains why a communist can defend the worst sort of evil as an innocent good. Whatever accelerates the dialectic of history, and thus hastens the day when communists will dominate the world, is virtuous.

Even children are tempted to think that power outranks love. They quarrel a good deal of the time. And when they quarrel, they pretend that they are busy defending the cause of truth. But they are really defending themselves. They are trying to seem better by making others seem worse.

V

But if a child expends so much energy quarreling, why does Jesus tell his disciples to imitate the manners of a child? The answer is quite within reach. A child may quarrel, thus betraying the work of original sin in his life. But when it comes right

43

down to it, he rests in love and not power. His quarreling is always a minor theme in his life; the major theme is love. At the end of the day, when the real ground of hope is defined, the child casts himself on the loving care of father and mother.

Knowledge brings power, and this power is good as far as it goes. But a child knows that it does not go far enough. The reason for this is not that the child does not know enough. The trouble lies in another direction. Knowledge cannot satisfy because it is impersonal in essence. It has neither life nor spirit.

But man has both life and spirit. This is why he must pass from knowledge to fellowship. Otherwise, he does not experience the release of love. A happy life is a shared life.

This in no way belittles the role of the intellect. A child cannot be happy unless he is consciously persuaded that he has parents, and that his parents love him. But the point is that the intellectual elements in this persuasion are subordinate to the vital elements. The *experience* of being loved, not an intellectual account of love, is the substance of a happy life.

VI

The Greeks realized that man cannot accept his own non-being. This is why they devised elaborate arguments for immortality. Nothing would be gained by reviewing these arguments, for it is enough to observe that they fail to the degree that they succeed. This is one of the grand ironies of Greek philosophy. Since the Greeks said that reason makes man most like the gods, they defined immortality as the liberation of reason from the prison of time and passion. Such liberation divested man of everything that makes him an individual. Let us develop this.

A human being is as much a hindrance to philosophic ideals as he is to scientific ideals, for neither philosophy nor science can take in the free, unpredictable aspects of a person. Philosophy can take in aspects that fall under universal man (such as the differentiae that separate man from the animals), while science can take in aspects that fall under natural law (such as the properties of skin or blood); but a person enjoys creative possibilities that are neither logical nor scientific. A freely inspired person plays tennis or sulks for the same reason that Socrates preferred to leave the fields and go into the market place. Human beings are unpredictable for the very reason that they are free.

Hence, if immortality means that man is divested of his individual traits, then immortality is death, not life. It is death because the sparkle and joy of personal existence, and thus the conditions for sharing life in the outgoing duties of love, are destroyed.

The Greeks managed to get on with it because they were governed by insights that were more native to the convictions of the heart than to the conclusions of philosophy. Socrates was a charming person to be around. But the charm flowed out of the free, creative possibilities of his life, and not out of the attributes that he had in common with the race. The same holds true for every charming person. A child discloses the uniqueness of his life by every smile and frown. And no loving parent would think of subordinating this uniqueness to the toneless generalizations of universal man.

VII

When the Apostle Paul examined the claims of wisdom, he drew a distinction between the wisdom of the world (intellectual detachment) and the wisdom of God (spiritual insight). "Where is the wise man? Where is the scribe? Where is the debater of this age? Has not God made foolish the wisdom of the world? For since, in the wisdom of God, the world did not know God through wisdom, it pleased God through the folly of what we preach to save those who believe" (I Corinthians 1:20-21).

But how could Paul make such a distinction? It is well known that philosophers have devoted more attention to the being and attributes of God than to any other subject. Moreover, Christian theologians have made a heavy draft upon this philosophic labor.

Paul would certainly grant that intellectual detachment can

reach correct conclusions about God. But this is not the same as *knowing* God. We only know a person when we are in fellowship with him, and fellowship does not exist until detachment gives way to commitment. Fellowship is a vital sharing of lives.

Neither Plato nor Aristotle saw any connection between a knowledge of God and a humble walk before God. Since they believed that man was most like the divine order when he was engaged in rational dialectic, they assumed that a fruitful knowledge of God could be gained by intellectual detachment. Plato's God was the efficient cause in creation, while Aristotle's God was the unmoved mover. Neither philosopher realized that detachment prejudices theology. It assumes that God is not a person; it then proceeds to draw inferences from this assumption.

This was by no means an innocent mistake, for it led to a loss of hope. Plato's God could not create a happy society because he was limited in power. He *wanted* to create a world without evil, but his intentions were frustrated by the limitations of matter. Matter would not yield to the perfection of the world of Ideas. And since God was not sovereign at the beginning of history, there was no reason to believe that he would be sovereign at the end. Where, then, was hope?

Aristotle's God was so transcendent that he did not even know that human beings existed. God was a metaphysical philosopher; he was absorbed in eternal self-reflection. God did not pity Aristotle, nor did he communicate assurances of hope, for intellectual detachment cannot pass from the universal to the particular. Aristotle's God knew mankind, but not Aristotle.

VIII

It is easy for detachment to conclude that when Martha and Mary said, "Lord, he whom you love is ill," the sisters were merely communicating a piece of information that could be added to man's ever-growing store of knowledge. They were doing this, to be sure, but their main purpose was to inspire duty, not to communicate knowledge. Friends already know the important things about one another, for they have shared their lives in fellowship. This is why the language of love can be brief. Love needs no more than a sign that the beloved is in distress. If a father learns that his child has been injured, he does not pause with circumstantials. He knows all he needs to know. Because he has united his life to that of the child, the cries of the child stir up a powerful sense of duty in his heart.

Detachment refuses to admit that love is a medium of knowledge. But this refusal is a sign of prejudice, for only love has access to those creative possibilities in a person which are richer and more intimate than either universal man or natural law. A person's secrets remain hidden until he chooses to reveal them, and he will only reveal them when he is treated as a person. Unless love opens the door to the heart, access is denied.

If we wish to know another person, we must walk up and ask in a friendly voice, "Hello, how are you?" When the person addressed is satisfied that his dignity is being received, he then is free to disclose his heart. The intimacy of the disclosure is governed by the intimacy of the trust. Friends tell many secrets, but lovers tell more.

Since an individual has many attributes that are common with the race, detachment can learn a great deal about man as man. And the information is useful in both philosophy and science. By remembering that our neighbor is a human being, we can go a long way in discharging the duties of love. We can use our common characteristics as a base for doing as we would be done by. We know that our neighbor does not want to be hurt, and we know that he wants food for dinner and not stones.

But detachment can never, in all eternity, discover the unique aspects of a person. Unless our neighbor chooses to reveal himself, the most interesting features of his life will remain concealed. And he will only reveal himself when he is sure that he is being treated as a person. Detachment must yield to trust.

This should not be difficult for philosophers to see, for they know that a neighbor has no access to *their* secrets until they choose to reveal themselves; and they will not make this choice

47

until the neighbor gives spiritual proofs that he can be entrusted with truth. No person will disclose his secrets if he suspects that the truth will be used against him.

The more we surrender our lives to one another in love and fellowship, the more intimately we know one another. And the intimacy grows in proportion to the purity of the trust. Thus, Jesus *knew* Lazarus because he *loved* him. It was on the strength of this knowledge that Martha and Mary sought to stir up a sense of duty in Jesus. They did not have to labor their point, as if Jesus were slow to respond. On the contrary, they used seven words to say all they had to say. They could be brief because they drew on all that Jesus knew by his long and happy association with Lazarus. Jesus *would* answer their call, for his great piety would prompt him to do as he would be done by. His heart would have no peace until he discharged the duties of love.

There is no level of life in which love fails to enlarge knowledge. The more we love a person, the more we know him. When a mother fondles her child, the very essence of the child leaps into her heart. The resulting union of natures is so perfect that the mother knows the child better than she knows herself.

IX

When we say that love is a medium of knowledge, we offend an honored axiom in the philosophic fraternity. Philosophers may disagree on many things, but they agree that there is only one medium of knowledge, and that is a critically disciplined intellect. In other words, truth is a property of self-consistent judgments, judgments that can be defended or refuted in a public forum. If a student has a working knowledge of the laws of inference, he is ready for business.

This assumes that intellectual detachment has access to all available information. But in truth, the most important information, that which involves the secrets of the heart, remains inaccessible until detachment gives way to fellowship. This is a rule to which there is no exception.

"But if love is a medium of knowledge," a philosopher retorts, "where *is* this knowledge? And what part does it play in the formation of a world view?" The very nature of such questions is proof that philosophy has limits. And if a philosopher would be a truly wise man, he should cheerfully submit to these limits. He should remind himself, not once or twice, but again and again, that there is no way in which the secrets of a person, whether of God or a neighbor, can be absorbed into a world view —no way, that is, without destroying the uniqueness of the person. Philosophic systems are confined to such generalizations as class concepts and universals. These systems can take in the essence of mankind, but not the essence of an individual. Yet, the most important object is the individual, not mankind as an abstraction.

But does this mean that philosophy is an invalid discipline? The answer is a resounding No! The issue is the *limits,* not the *rights,* of philosophy. And if we proceed with caution, it will be seen that the rights are preserved by a cheerful submission to the limits.

As long as a philosopher remembers that he is a human being whose secrets remain his own until he chooses to reveal them, he will be delivered from the error of thinking that love has no role to play in the task of gaining knowledge. And how does a philosopher keep such a fact before him? By imitating the manners of a happy child, as Jesus advises. A child does not prejudice the possibilities of reality by intellectual detachment. He is content to accept things as they are.

And what is reality? It is exactly what our hearts confront in the daily affairs of life. When a philosopher drinks coffee in the philosophic fraternity, or when he embraces his wife and children, he knows what is real. He is able to enter into spiritual realities, for he tempers detachment with love. His intellectual life is firm because his moral life is firm.

49

A virtuous philosopher may never be celebrated as an original philosopher. But he will be praised as a good man who inspires good students. Having reminded himself that intellectual detachment becomes perverse whenever it usurps the office of love, he will make it his duty to remind others, too. "The fear of the Lord is the beginning of wisdom" (Psalm 111:10).

CHAPTER FOUR

Jesus Cares for His Own

"And thank Heaven, fasting, for a good man's love."
— Shakespeare

When Martha and Mary sent for Jesus, they appealed to his great love. And their appeal was well directed. "Now Jesus loved Martha and her sister and Lazarus" (John 11:5). Love implies a vital sharing of natures. It is a habit of life, born of the convictions of the heart, which prompts a person to do as he would be done by. All people crave signs that they are needed and wanted. Love cheerfully gives these signs.

Love does all it can to remove barriers to fellowship. It eases strained relations; it resists boasting and pretense. Happy children bear witness to the pleasures that love brings. As long as they know they are needed and wanted, they cast themselves on life in a relaxed, carefree manner.

Since love has extraordinary powers of adaptability, it needs no handbook of morals to guide it. It simply adjusts its response to the situation. A gentle smile relieves the fear of censure, a pat on the back encourages manliness. Love is always appreciative; it listens or speaks when the moment is right; it is never patronizing.

When love confronts uncertainties, it waits on the disclosure of life that fellowship brings. It allows others to express their native feelings, preferences, or motives. With this new information in hand, love can be more precise in doing as it would be done by.

I

The manners of love begin with small, delicate assurances that others are human beings, made in the image of God. These assurances include courtesy, tact, helpful gestures, and timely words of encouragement. As long as the small duties of love are honored, the large duties will take care of themselves. If a person waxes eloquent on cosmic tasks, when he refuses to be kind to his own neighbor, he is a hypocrite.

Discourtesy is the first sign that a person is unwilling to honor the dignity of man. All other evils begin with this evil. Even murder is an expression of selfishness.

When love grows into personal affection, the resulting union of natures is so intimate that the heart recoils at the very thought of wounding the beloved. It was on the strength of this intimacy that Martha and Mary sent for Jesus. While Jesus loved all men (he always did as he would be done by), he had a special affection for his friends. Affection is not possible unless personalities are compatible, and compatibility is not easy to come by in this life.

Even Samuel Johnson overlooked the difference between love and affection. On one occasion Mrs. Knowles said to him, "We are commanded to do good to all men, 'but especially to them who are of the household of Faith.'" To which Johnson replied, "Well, Madam, the household of Faith is wide enough." Mrs. Knowles rejoined, "But, Doctor, our Saviour had twelve Apostles, yet there was *one* whom he *loved*. John was called 'the disciple whom Jesus loved.'" Johnson replied, with eyes sparkling benignantly, "Very well, indeed, Madam. You have said very well." Boswell remarked, "A fine application. Pray, Sir, had you ever thought of it?"[1] Johnson admitted that he had not.

Scripture says that Jesus went about doing good. His entire life was dedicated to serving others. He loved God with all his heart, and his neighbor as himself. "Our Lord's mode of doing good sets forth His incessant activity! He did not only the good which came close to hand, but he 'went about' on His errands of mercy. Throughout the whole land of Judea there was scarcely a village or hamlet which was not gladdened by the sight of him."[2] No man ever drew near to Jesus but that Jesus gave gentle, spiritual signs that his life was precious in the sight of God. Jesus was always sincere, and he asked for nothing but sincerity in return. He never stooped to dissimulation or guile; his true self was always on display. He spoke with the charm of a child, yet with the wisdom of God. He risked everything on love. If the circuit of fellowship was cut, it was cut by those who refused his summons. He never set up legal barriers between himself and others.

Since we are born with a restless urge to count, only love can satisfy our hearts. If others accept us because of something we possess, or because of some influence we can exert on their behalf, we are not accepted for what we are. Were it not for the power that we happen to enjoy, we would be rejected. This is why Jesus would not entrust himself to those who sought to make him king. He knew what was in their hearts. Rather than receiving him as Lord and Saviour, they wanted to use him as an instrument for their own will-to-power.

II

Lazarus was a nonentity in the eyes of the world, yet Jesus loved him. This should cheer our hearts, for most of us have little standing in this life. Obscurity is painful because it im-

[1]Boswell, *Life of Johnson,* Britannica Great Books ed., Vol. 44, p. 392. Used by permission.

[2]Charles Spurgeon, *Morning and Evening Daily Devotions* (Zondervan), p. 220. Used by permission.

plies that we are not interesting; and all of us want to be interesting. This is why we strive to be accepted by others.

The world may love the powerful and the rich, but Jesus takes up residence in a meek and thankful heart. He thoroughly enjoyed his visits to Bethany. Lazarus did not have to put on airs, for Jesus took him as he was.

If Lazarus symbolizes the pain of personal obscurity, Martha and Mary symbolize the pain of personal peculiarities. For example, the Evangelist Luke tells of an incident that happened when Jesus stopped at Bethany for fellowship. The personal peculiarities of the sisters emerged in a striking way. Martha, the anxious hostess, was busy serving; while Mary, contemplative and retiring, sat at Jesus' feet. All went well until Martha discovered that Mary was getting more attention. Inwardly pained, Martha determined to do something about the situation. So, she went to Jesus and tattled on Mary. "Lord, do you not care that my sister has left me to serve alone? Tell her then to help me" (Luke 10:40).

It is quite possible that Martha did not realize she was tattling. Since we are not always aware of our true motives, she may have thought she was merely redressing an injustice. Was it fair for her to do all the work?

But Jesus knew that she was really trying to call attention to herself. "But the Lord answered her, 'Martha, Martha, you are anxious and troubled about many things; one thing is needful. Mary has chosen the good portion, which shall not be taken away from her'" (v. 41). Jesus would not let Martha shift the norm of acceptance from love to power. But he did this in such a way that Martha had no reason to wilt, nor Mary to gloat. He pitied the sisters, for neither had final control over personal peculiarities.

III

When children quarrel, they are trying to prove their worth as individuals. They strive to get ahead of each other. But the striving is self-defeating, for it pushes kindness and truth into the background. This makes it all the more difficult for love to have its perfect way.

The same thing is true in life. If a man tries to prove his worth by getting power over others, he takes a fatal course; for every boast he makes can be countered by an even greater boast. A plucky neighbor can earn more money, buy a larger house, or join a more fashionable club. Once an individual enters the heated race for competitive status, the soul knows no rest. "All things are full of weariness; a man cannot utter it; the eye is not satisfied with seeing, nor the ear filled with hearing" (Ecclesiastes 1:8).

Jesus warned that it is easier for a camel to pass through the eye of a needle than for a rich man to enter the kingdom of heaven. All men are invited to enter this kingdom, but not all men accept the invitation. When a rich man looks to his possessions for security, he announces, as it were, that he can dispense with divine mercies. He is deceived, for in the end his soul will be required by God. "There is a way which seems right to a man, but its end is the way to death" (Proverbs 14:12).

Unless the soul takes periodic inventory of its reason for existence, it may exhaust its strength on things that will afford no consolation when health is lost or when death knocks at the door. Power brings admirers, but it does not make friends. And without friendship we surrender hope, for the kingdom of love forms the outer court of the kingdom of heaven.

When Jesus told his disciples to imitate the manners of a happy child, he practiced what he preached. Simplicity and contentment were steady characteristics of his life. He had no employment, owned no real estate, and often lived by the charity of his friends. Still, he never suffered feelings of insecurity, for he completed his life in the love of his heavenly Father.

We have not been called to follow the Lord in the duties that pertain to his office as Saviour. But we *have* been called to live a meek and thankful life. A charitable person will not only hold his goods lightly, but he will invite others to share in the use of these goods. Love makes everyone feel at home.

IV

When a child is deprived of the security that love brings, he may revolt against those who reject him. Parents often give their children the impression that acceptance is decided by such standards as proficiency in school or leadership in the neighborhood. A legal spirit replaces love. As a result, the children must always be on guard. They may be ready to tell the truth about themselves, but they are afraid they will not be approved. As the ties of trust deteriorate, the little ones not only lose respect for their parents, but they are robbed of their sense of dignity. How can they feel clean and upright, when their own parents will not trust them?

Samuel Butler satirizes the hypocrisy of patronizing parents: "To parents who wish to lead a quiet life I would say: Tell your children that they are very naughty — much naughtier than most children. Point to the young people of some acquaintances as models of perfection and impress your own children with a deep sense of their own inferiority. You carry so many more guns than they do that they cannot fight you. This is called moral influence, and it will enable you to bounce them as much as you please. . . . Tell them how singularly indulgent you are; insist on the incalculable benefit you conferred upon them, firstly in bringing them into the world at all, but more particularly in bringing them into it as your own children rather than as anyone else's. Say that you have their highest interests at stake whenever you are out of temper and wish to make yourself unpleasant by way of balm to your soul. Harp much upon these highest interests."[3]

The extremes of youthful rebellion are illustrated by the juvenile delinquent. Since the delinquent does not know why he feels insecure, his conduct is random and erratic. He only

[3]*The Way of All Flesh* (Oxford), pp. 26-27. Used by permission.

knows that he cannot measure up to prevailing social standards. So, he recovers a sense of adequacy by joining a gang. He is resentful against a world that does not accept him, and that he in turn does not accept.

But the security of the gang proves spurious, for in turning against the conventions of society, the delinquent also turns against the duties of love. In the end, all reassuring standards are demolished. The delinquent cannot tell the truth about himself, lest others discover how insecure he really is. He must wear a mask; he submits to his comrades out of fear.

A poorly managed home is the cradle of juvenile delinquency. When children are not approved, they are deprived of the wisdom that only love can bring. As a result, they are deceived into thinking that security comes from power rather than love. They embark on life with a spurious standard of selfhood.

Even when parents think they are doing well by their children, they sometimes overlook the most elementary signs of love. Take discipline, for example. Children are not secure unless they are told how far they can go. When they imagine that they are self-sufficient, they not only get into trouble by rebelling against authority, but they load their hearts with anxiety by having to make decisions which are beyond their depth.

A cruel and unfeeling society takes over where a poorly managed home leaves off. Society says that the secure man, the one to be envied and emulated, is the one who enjoys power, not the one who is kind and truthful. Persuaded by this propaganda, a delinquent is seized by a spirit of covetousness. He determines to get power by fair means or foul. And when he fails to get the power he seeks, or when he gets the power but fails to get satisfaction from it, he becomes all the more desperate. In a flight from the self he may turn to narcotics, liquor, or sex. But rather than restoring a sense of personal adequacy, each new perversity becomes a cruel taskmaster. When freedom is surrendered, personal dignity is surrendered.

Hardness of heart may eventually dull the delinquent's sense of right and wrong. Sometimes this process leads to what is the most irrational thrust of all. A delinquent may commit a crime out of ceremonial indifference. The crime is so utterly senseless that society *must* pay attention to him. But this brief exposure to the public eye brings no satisfaction. The cup of despair lies nearby.

A prostitute is said to be in the world's oldest profession. When she begins her depraved career, she may imagine that she will enjoy power over the male, and that this power will give her real security. But she errs. Since she is joined to her clients by money rather than love, she does not accept them and they do not accept her. Many prostitutes share their income with a pimp. A pimp helps alleviate insecurity in two ways. First, he gives the prostitute an illusion of relative virtue, for his degradation is worse than hers. Second, he may be the only one with whom she can share the truth about herself. In this case he is the last stopping place between her way of life and the outer darkness of total rejection. This is one reason why the suicide rate is high among prostitutes. When a female has surrendered her blushing innocence, she does not have much left.

V

It is ironic, however, that when people fall into gross social sins, they are often more willing to be honest before God, and thus to repent of their sins, than the proud and mighty of this world. Jesus was aware of this irony. "Truly, I say to you, the tax collectors and the harlots go into the kingdom of God before you" (Matthew 21:31). The delinquent and the prostitute may transgress the laws of God, but they do not use these laws to justify themselves. They have fallen short of the glory of God, and they are honest enough to say so. If they cannot hide their sins from man, how can they hide them from God?

Jesus reserved his severest judgment for those who were guilty but sought to cover their guilt with the garments of self-right-eousness. "You blind guides," he said to the scribes and Phari-sees, "straining out a gnat and swallowing a camel!" (Matthew 23:24). Hypocrisy removes the severity of the divine law, and thus the need for personal repentance, by substituting petty ceremonies for the heights of self-giving love. When the Pharisee stood in the temple of God, he was thankful that he was not like other men. He imagined that he was exempt from divine judgment. The publican would not so much as look up into heaven, but smote his breast in remorse. The publican went away justified; he enjoyed the fruits of evangelical repentance.

Since a self-righteous person is more concerned with power than he is with love, he has little pity for those who fall by the way. In the parable of the Good Samaritan the priest and the Levite were too occupied with official duties to be kind to a neighbor. Even service to God can be corrupted into an excuse for serving the self rather than God.

VI

Psychotherapy has confronted modern man with new proof that love is the law of life. A person's hunger for approval can become so great that he may fall into psychic distress. Only love can detect the symptoms of this disease, and effect a cure. Freud brought this needed love. He restored the symbolism of common grace by accepting the unacceptable. Neurotic behavior evoked scorn from society, judgment from the church. Freud rejected both attitudes. He refused to believe that neurotics were either odd or perverse. They were sick, that was all.

Through a series of painstaking studies, Freud discovered that neurotics are victims of forces of which they are not conscious, and over which they have neither moral nor rational control. He made this discovery because he restored the ethic of honesty in human relations. He created a spiritual bond between himself and his patients. He was not shocked by anything divulged through free association. He never sat in judgment; he maintained clinical detachment.

In other words, Freud helped neurotics by treating them as persons. When his patients experienced acceptance, they had courage to confront areas of the psyche that were repressed because of ignorance or fear. Freud was wise enough to see that nothing would be gained by preaching to neurotics.

Psychotherapy proves that many people are ready to deal with the less pleasant aspects of their lives, but they are not sure how to go about doing it. There are few people, Christian or otherwise, who can be entrusted with an intimate disclosure of the heart.

Honesty in human relations is much scarcer than we realize, especially when shameful things must be dealt with. The existing social order is held together by cords of deception. We will not tell others what we think of them, nor will we allow them to tell what they think of us. So, we compromise. We will be honest, but not so honest as to seem peculiar.

Deception tinctures even the most intimate human relations. A female does not understand the male's sensual appetites, nor does the male understand the female's craving for tender affection. Partial understanding is all we can expect. Male and female will baffle each other until the end of time. In the exchange of the marital due, neither partner reveals the extent to which erotic pleasure is intensified by fantasy.

When we remember how hard it is to be honest in sexual matters, we are not surprised that Freud found a close connection between sexual repression and emotional illness. Victorian society entertained such prudish standards that many people, especially women, were afraid they would be rejected if their true feelings became known.

But the problem is by no means confined to Victorian times. Sexual drives can serve as engines of anxiety in *any* society. These drives not only offend prudery, but they suggest conduct that raises a blush in our better faculties. If we were to gratify all our sexual drives, society would disintegrate.

VII

Freud recovered the ethic of honesty on one level of life, but in so doing he also pointed up what we may call the paradox of existence. We cannot be happy unless we are honest about ourselves, for love only thrives in an atmosphere of trust. But we can never be perfectly sure how others will receive the truth about our lives, especially when we divulge shameful things. We may be ridiculed; we may be tattled on. Who knows?

Freud admitted that he had no solution to the paradox of existence. "My courage fails me, therefore, at the thought of rising up as a prophet before my fellow-men, and I bow to their reproach that I have no consolation to offer them."[4] Freud said that about all we can do is to arrange our illusions in such a way that we experience the greatest pleasure and the least pain.

Freud knew that society can be dreadfully cruel. It forces people to repress their natural desires, and thus to burden the unconscious centers of the psyche with all sorts of unfulfilled wishes. But he knew of no way to circumvent the problem. If society did not subdue the mutinous impulses in human nature, all decent relations, including those of the fraternity of psychology, would collapse. Murder and rape could be justified as expressions of natural instinct.

Freud could not articulate a philosophy of hope because he could not break from scientific detachment. This detachment helped him restore the ethic of honesty when dealing with neurotics, but it kept him from understanding the relationship between hope and the duties of love in normal people. After helping a neurotic recover the gentle voice of reason, Freud was at the end of his tether. The patient was returned to society, there to take his place in a highly competitive order that leaves little room for the ethic of honesty.

It seems that Freud did not make the best use of his discoveries as therapist. Rather than defining love as a vital sharing of natures, and so connecting it with his own act of accepting the unacceptable, he linked it with genital expression. If he had paid more attention to the spiritual elements in love, and less to the biological, he might have understood that man has creative possibilities that transcend the pleasure-seeking "id."

4*Civilization and Its Discontents,* Britannica Great Books ed., Vol. 54, p. 802. Used by permission of the Hogarth Press, London.

VIII

Although Freud made no profession of faith in Christ, he nonetheless defended the very reason why such faith is good and proper. He proved that people will only deal with the perverse areas of their hearts, and thus experience acceptance, when they are treated as human beings — in other words, when they are loved.

Whereas Freud confined his interests to neurotics, Jesus opened the way for all men to come to the light, and so be healed. Jesus received others just as they were; he made it easy for them to be honest with themselves and with God. He never used their transgressions as evidence of his own virtue, nor was he ever rudely unapproachable. He wore modest clothing, possessed few goods, and spoke a simple but comforting message. From the beginning of his ministry to the end, he defended love as the highest norm of virtue and the true pathway to happiness.

Jesus is the light of the world, for in his very person he fulfilled all righteousness. He brought human nature to perfection by loving God with all his heart, and his neighbor as himself. We measure our own distance from righteousness by drawing near to him. And since he came to reveal the love of God, we are able to rejoice in his perfection, and to repent of our own imperfection. He assures us that God will receive us just as we are, without one plea. He teaches us how to enjoy the security that comes from living an open and transparent life. God not only knows all that is in our heart, but he loves us despite what he knows. It was out of a pity for sinners that the Father sent the Son to be the propitiation for the world.

Jesus' great love for sinners is illustrated by his conversation with the woman at the well. Although the woman was living in adultery, Jesus did not make a frontal attack on her transgressions. He did not even make sin the first topic of inquiry. His goal was to *win* her, not to *condemn* her; and to reach this goal he had to assure her that she would not be rejected because she was a sinner. So, he opened the conversation by asking for a drink. But the woman was taken aback. She wondered how he, a Jew, would presume to speak to her, a Samaritan. Jesus was not offended. Having put himself in her place, he knew how she felt. Moreover, he was pleased with her forthrightness. She let him know where he stood. Honesty is the first step toward trust.

After Jesus won the woman's confidence, he then went on to reveal her sin. But he did it with such artistry that the woman was able to accept the truth about herself without fear that she would be rejected for doing so. Jesus disarmed her with his great love. She knew she was in the presence of one who sought to help her, not judge her.

In the end, the woman's heart melted. Love had its perfect way. She not only confessed that Jesus was a prophet of God, but she went on to acknowledge him as the Messiah. With the burden of sin lifted, the woman felt so relieved that in a burst of joy she ran off to tell others. "So the woman left her water jar, and went away into the city, and said to the people, 'Come, see a man who told me all that I ever did. Can this be the Christ?'" (John 4:28-29).

IX

Jesus taught his followers to worship God in spirit and in truth. In this manner he brought the ethic of honesty to its highest form. When a sinner worships God, he shows that he is willing to have God scrutinize everything in his heart. Nothing is concealed, all is revealed. "Let the words of my mouth and the meditation of my heart be acceptable in thy sight, O Lord, my rock and my redeemer" (Psalm 19:14). This is the way a sinner prays when he is delivered from the fear that God will reject him because he is not worthy to stand in the presence of God. Christ paid the full debt of sin. All God asks is that we repent of our sins.

When we are persuaded that God loves us, we have a norm by which to deal with the problem of rejection in society. If others are not kind to us, we are able to pity them, for we know that but for the grace of God we would do the same thing. And if we fail to be kind to others, we are restored to righteousness by meditating on the law of God. Being forgiven by God, we are encouraged to live a more consistent life before our neighbor.

A forgiven sinner neither boasts nor despairs. He can accept present insecurity on the assurance that God has promised something better for all who love him. "For this slight momentary affliction is preparing for us an eternal weight of glory beyond all comparison" (II Corinthians 4:17). As long as we are accepted by God, we can bear human rejection in hope and patience.

Although modern psychology has not come as far as Christ, it has nevertheless gone considerable distance beyond Freud. Many therapists recognize that man has a moral defect in his will and in his affections. This defect prompts man to do and say things that he regrets. And what other term can designate this self-destructive tendency, save *sin?* Sin is much more serious than a conflict between the pleasure principle and social restrictions. It is a spiritual admission that the self is out of harmony with its own essence.

When we suffer from emotional illness, we should turn to psychotherapy. Psychic distress is not a moral issue. But when we suffer from a feeling of alienation from God, we should turn to the Lord, for only the Lord has authority to forgive sins and to reconcile us to our Maker.

CHAPTER FIVE

The Problem of Evil

"If this is the best of all possible worlds, what are the others like?"
— Voltaire

Although Jesus knew that Lazarus was near death, he did not hasten to Bethany. Instead, he purposely waited until Lazarus died. "So when he heard that he was ill, he stayed two days longer in the place where he was" (John 11:6). There is no doubt that Jesus purposely waited, for if he had wanted to save Lazarus, he certainly could have done so. On some occasions he merely *spoke* and the sick were cured.

Jesus' delay points up a delicate moral issue. We believe that if a physician purposely withheld medicine until his patient died, he would be charged with dereliction of duty. Was Jesus exempt from standards that bind upright men in society?

The issue is delicate because it touches a problem that has haunted men from the very dawn of culture. This is the problem of evil. If God is able to deliver us from suffering, why do we suffer so much? Is *God* exempt from standards that bind upright men in society?

65

I

Many and eloquent are the descriptions of the problem of evil. "We come into the world in weakness, and in a case in which we cannot help ourselves, but are a pity and trouble to others. We are their trouble that breed us and bring us up. We are vexed with unsatisfied desires, with troubling passions, with other tormenting pains, with languishing weakness, and enemies' malice; with poverty and care; with losses and crosses, and shame and grief; with hard labour and studies; with the injuries and spectacles of a bedlam world, and with fears of death, and death at last."[1]

The problem of evil has shattered the faith of many. Darwin said he could not believe in a personal God because "there seems to me too much misery in the world." Nature and man are often in moral disagreement. "In sober truth," cries John Stuart Mill, "nearly all the things which men are hanged or imprisoned for doing to one another, are nature's every day performances. Killing, the most criminal act recognized by human laws, Nature does once to every being that lives; and in a large proportion of cases, after protracted tortures such as only the greatest monsters whom we read of ever purposely inflicted on their living fellow-creatures. . . . Nature impales men, breaks them as if on the wheel, casts them to be devoured by wild beasts, burns them to death, crushes them with stones like the first Christian martyr, starves them with hunger, freezes them with cold, poisons them by the quick or slow venom of her exhalations, and has hundreds of other hideous deaths in reserve, such as the ingenious cruelty of a Nabis or a Domitian never surpassed. All this, Nature does with the most supercilious disregard both of mercy and of justice, emptying her shafts upon the best and noblest indifferently with the meanest and worst; those who are engaged in the highest and worthiest enterprises,

[1]Richard Baxter, *The Reasons of the Christian Religion*, Part I, Chapter XI.

and often as the direct consequence of the noblest acts; and it might almost be imagined as a punishment for them."[2]

Even men of faith have been baffled by the problem of evil. Cried Jeremiah, "Righteous art thou, O Lord, when I complain to thee; yet I would plead my case before thee. Why does the way of the wicked prosper? Why do all who are treacherous thrive?" (12:1). Cried the Psalmist, "For I was envious of the arrogant, when I saw the prosperity of the wicked. For they have no pangs; their bodies are sound and sleek. They are not in trouble as other men are; they are not stricken like other men" (73:3-5).

Concern for the problem of evil is not necessarily a sign of unbelief. Rather, it may be a sign that a person is trying to earn his right to believe. Cheap faith either does not see the problem of evil, or it sees it but makes nothing of it. Hardness of heart is the father of cheap faith, for who can learn that a child has been born blind, or that a tornado has ripped through a sleeping village, without wondering why God allows such frightful things to happen?

Since God is a God of mercy, he is willing to hold conversation with those who *want* to believe but who have difficulty believing. For example, Habakkuk shows a holy boldness when he brings the problem of evil to God's attention. "Thou who art of purer eyes than to behold evil and canst not look on wrong, why dost thou look on faithless men, and art silent when the wicked swallows up the man more righteous than he?" (1:13). Habakkuk is a troubled child, not a calculating skeptic. God patiently listens to his complaint.

Job took hold of the problem of evil, and he would not let go until he found a reason for his suffering. "God has made my heart faint; the Almighty has terrified me; for I am hemmed in by darkness, and thick darkness covers my face" (23:16-17). The darkness was so impenetrable that Job was ready to parley with God. "Oh, that I knew where I might find him, that I might come even to his seat! I would lay my case before him

2*Three Essays on Religion*, pp. 28-29.

and fill my mouth with arguments. I would learn what he would answer me, and understand what he would say to me" (23:3-5). Since Job was not always careful to respect the majesty of God, he incurred discipline. But God dealt with him as a child needing correction, not as a criminal deserving punishment.

II

Although many approaches to the problem of evil have been devised, only four have stood the test of time: (1) we despair of a solution and become skeptics; (2) we say that good and evil form an eternal dualism; (3) we postulate a pantheism in which evil is either an illusion or an instrumental good; (4) we rest in the sovereignty of God. The first possibilities — skepticism and dualism — do not commend themselves to the heart, for they destroy the very *possibility* of hope. Skepticism has no assurance that life will end happily, while dualism says that the conflict between good and evil will continue forever. How, then, can a pious heart have hope?

On the other hand, faith in the sovereignty of God seems to leave the present conflict between good and evil unexplained. If God is all-good and all-powerful, why did he create this kind of a world in the first place? For these and other reasons pantheism has commended itself to the minds of many.

Christian Science is a popular form of pantheism. It starts with the major premise that God is all in all. From this it deduces the conclusion that evil has no reality. Evil is an illusion of the material sense, and a prudent man ought to regard it as such.

This argument sounds plausible, but in truth it is a tissue of fallacies. In all the world there is nothing more real than pain. The experience of a crushed finger enters consciousness with a force surpassing that of Euclid's geometry. Now, if we cannot trust our senses when we suffer pain, how much less can we trust them when Christian Science says that pain is an illusion? Not only is the suffering much more vivid than the lecture on Christian Science, but the lecture is conveyed to the mind

68

through the very channels of sense-perception that Christian Science says we cannot trust. The position refutes itself.

Philosophical pantheism views the universe as either an emanation from God, or as God considered under various modal aspects. But both possibilities are unacceptable, and every child knows why. If God and the universe are the same thing, then human beings are not human beings at all. They are aspects of God. But this is false. Human beings are sinners, and sin has no place in the divine being.

Spinoza argued that we have no right to believe that the universe is friendly to human values. He defined the universe as a vast order of necessary being, something like a huge triangle.

This is all well and good, but just try telling it to a child. A child knows that if nature is like a huge triangle, then Spinoza himself is part of this triangle. In this case Spinoza is not free to go for a walk, let alone draw up a system of pantheism. Triangles are governed by the laws of geometry. They have no power of contrary choice.

Leibniz dismissed pantheism, but his own approach to the problem of evil was no more fruitful. After acknowledging the reality of evil in the world, he then went on to say that evil is a necessary element in the best of all possible worlds. Evil is an instrumental good; it promotes a system of divine justice. Leibniz called this system a "theodicy."

Voltaire attacked the theodicy in his brilliant satire *Candide*. And since his attack was cast in the form of man's dramatic conflict between good and evil, he unwittingly drew on the convictions of the heart. His readers identified themselves with the hero. This is why Voltaire was so devastating. No child could believe that the Lisbon earthquake was an example of distributive justice. Why did the people of Lisbon suffer, when others, equally undeserving, were spared? God may have permitted the earthquake for reasons that we cannot name. But this is far different from saying that the catastrophe promoted justice in the world.

On several occasions Jesus reminded his disciples that God's ways are not our ways, nor his thoughts our thoughts. He said that the Tower of Siloam did not fall on those who were greater sinners than others (Luke 13:4-5). This is convincing evidence that we cannot solve the problem of evil on the single principle of theodicy. There is mystery in Providence.

Again, when Jesus' disciples inquired about the man born blind, they were told that "it was not that this man sinned, or his parents, but that the works of God might be manifest in him" (John 9:3). Here is more mystery.

A pious heart is ready to accept mystery, for we are men and not God. Neither science nor philosophy can penetrate the reasons for Providence. Unless God tells us why he made this world, we shall go to our graves in ignorance.

What, then, is the resolution? The resolution is that we should walk humbly before God. As long as we live meek and thankful lives, God will give us signs that we count. The resulting joy will deliver us from an excessive preoccupation with the problem of evil. And even more, the elements of mystery in Providence will provoke a sense of pleasure in our heart, for they will serve as daily reminders that our lives are ordered by sovereign wisdom. If God is for us, who can be against us?

Voltaire successfully refuted Leibniz, but he did little to solve the problem of evil, let alone give us a reason for our hope. He exhausted his talents on the easy business of destruction. He not only ridiculed the theodicy, but he ridiculed the very idea of Providence itself. He treated virtue and vice with contemptuous indifference. In his zeal to refute a spurious system of justice, he sealed off the doorway to the kingdom of heaven; for if we cannot rest in the power and wisdom of God, we are undone. We are defenseless against senility and death.

III

As we reflect on the problem of evil, one important observation must be made. *When it comes to it, the convictions of the heart ask no more than the final triumph of goodness.* We establish this by noting the manner in which a child judges the conflict between good and evil in a fairy tale. The convictions of the heart do not rebel until it appears that good people are defeated. A child cannot accept such a defeat, for it implies his own defeat. He knows that if good people do not count, then he does not count; and his heart will have none of that. The kingdom of love is a kingdom of order, not confusion.

If we fail to humble ourselves and become like a child, we may lose sight of the real issue. The conflict between good and evil is a given fact. We have no power to change this fact, for we came into the world without consultation and we shall leave it in the same way. All we can do is trust and obey.

A child knows that Cinderella did not ask to be raised by her wicked stepmother, nor did she choose to live in poverty and neglect. She simply found herself in certain conditions, as does every child. And though there was little she could do about these conditions, there was one thing she could do about herself. She could choose to be good. And once she made this choice, she enjoyed the benefits of the kingdom of love. She had peace of heart, even though things about her were going wrong.

God created the world for reasons that are sufficient unto himself. It is not necessary that we be told these reasons. As long as we know that God loves us, we have a base for hope. And when we have hope, all else can be borne in patience. The important issue is settled.

If we harden our hearts and say that God had no right to create a world into which sickness and death should come, we destroy hope by entertaining attitudes of distrust. Distrust is worse than the problem of evil, for it cuts us off from fellowship with God. No person will disclose his secrets until the dignity of his life is respected. And if this is true in the case of man, is it any less true in the case of God?

This means that the problem of evil is not a critical problem unless it nullifies the assurance that our lives are precious in the sight of God. But as long as we are kind and truthful, this will never happen; for God promises to exalt all who humble themselves.

IV

Even though a child cannot solve the problem of evil, he does not give up hope. Nor does he found his hope upon credulousness. The little one rests in good and sufficient evidences, though these evidences will only commend themselves to people who stay in tune with the convictions of the heart. As long as a child feels needed and wanted, he believes that things will work out happily in the end.

When Anne Frank wrote her inspiring *Diary,* the convictions of the heart united with the promises of the Old Testament. Even though she saw evidences of brutality all about her, she refused to believe that brutality would have the last word. She was confident that the Lord was a friend of all who put their trust in him.

Happy children would say that Anne Frank was right. They have no idea how evil got into the world, nor are they much disturbed by this lack of knowledge. The important thing is how life *ends,* not how it *began.* All fairy tales are built around this order of values.

If we live by the wisdom that illuminates the heart of a child, we shall not become depressed by the problem of evil. We shall be content to rest in the sovereignty of God. As long as we know that God loves us, we can leave everything else to Providence.

When a child wants life to end happily, he is not being selfish. He wants a happy ending because he identifies himself with the fortunes of those who are good. This identification is a work of love, not an expression of selfishness; for what the child wishes for himself, he wishes for all who are good. The reference is universal.

In sum, a happy child does not suspend hope until he solves the problem of evil. In fact, he sees no connection between the two issues. Anne Frank was too busy enjoying herself to worry about cosmology. She was quite content to let the Lord run the universe. Jesus says that we should go and do likewise.

V

A detached intellect can raise all sorts of objections to a child's philosophy of hope. Thus, if Socrates were to meet Cinderella, he could bring her to tears by his relentless demand for self-consistent definitions. But in this semantic struggle, children would side with Cinderella. They would say that Socrates has no right to question things that are self-evident. Isn't Cinderella kind and truthful? What better definition of virtue could Socrates want?

A child does not lose hope unless he loses love. And he can lose love in two separate ways: when others reject him, or when he rejects others. When others reject him, he can compensate by seeking out his friends in the kingdom of love. He can talk to his pet, or he can invoke any number of imaginary playmates. As long as the child is good, hope glows brightly in his heart.

When the child rejects others, his own heart tells him how to set things right. He must seek forgiveness. And when he has done this, the kingdom of love puts no further obligations upon him. The duties of love are fulfilled by works of love.

A loving child lives and moves and has his being in God. "God is love, and he who abides in love abides in God, and God abides in him" (I John 4:16). A loving child would no more question the ground of hope than he would the beauty of a rose or the joy of a mother's kiss. He is *certain* that good people have nothing to fear, and what could be more certain than certain?

VI

Whenever we become so preoccupied with the problem of evil that we lose hope, we have drifted from the duties of love. Or at least we have lost sight of the benefits that accompany these duties. Humbling ourselves like a child is not something that we do once for all. It is a spiritual exercise through which we must pass each day. Otherwise, our hearts may harden.

A happy child is not anxious about the problem of evil. As long as he dwells in the kingdom of love, he has a base from which to *enjoy* life, not *worry* about it. He is content to let others do the worrying.

This means that a child has implicit faith in the sovereignty of God, for only God is able to deliver good people from the jaws of death. And because a child trusts in divine deliverance, he believes that God had good and sufficient reasons for making the present world.

A child is curious about the problem of evil, to be sure. He would like to sit with Job and Habakkuk, there to hear what God would say. But he puts no pressure on God. God can take all the time he wants, for friends know when to speak and when to be silent. And until the happy day when God tells why he made this kind of a world, a happy child goes about his affairs in the kingdom of love.

Little children were quick to make friends with Jesus, for they were drawn by his great love. And when he said he came from God to prepare a home for his friends, they believed him. They knew that it is wrong to distrust a good person, especially when this person knows what he is talking about. And Jesus was an expert on kingdom matters, for he proceeded from the very bosom of the Father.

If a person renounces his citizenship in the kingdom of love, he is denied a wisdom that proceeds from the heart. This makes him prey to despair. He no longer recognizes truths that are self-evident to children. As he drifts farther and farther from the convictions of the heart, the problem of evil becomes more acute. In the end he may deny the existence of God, or he may deny that God is all-good and all-powerful. Hope is lost in either case, for man does not have resources to save himself.

VII

Martha and Mary were disappointed when Jesus failed to reach Bethany in time, but they did not let this disappointment come between them and the Lord. Love is a steady relationship; it is not a series of fits and starts. Jesus was their friend, and as their friend he had a right to explain himself in a friendly atmosphere.

This means that the problem of evil served as a fresh occasion for Martha and Mary to sit at the feet of Jesus. Since *he* had chosen to delay his arrival, he alone could explain the reasons for this delay. In the meantime the sisters had one duty, and that was to be good.

Martha and Mary continued to hope, even though outwardly there seemed to be little reason to hope. They wept when Lazarus died, but they did not despair. They knew that sooner or later all men must die. And since they passed their days in the fear of God, they were persuaded that God would reunite loved ones in the kingdom of heaven.

If a person despairs of eternal life, the trouble may trace to himself. Let us illustrate what we mean. Darwin said that if he had his life to live over, he would make it a rule to read some poetry and listen to some music at least every week. He found that by neglecting his aesthetic faculty, he could not judge beauty effectively. The trouble was not a lack of beauty in the world, but a lack of appreciation in Darwin himself. Similarly, if a person fails to improve the convictions of the heart, he may lose hope. But his loss may trace to a lack of spiritual appreciation, and not to a lack of evidence that God will give eternal life to all who repent.

Hardness of heart tends to make an all-controlling issue out of the problem of evil. It contends that if *one* infant is born deformed, the intellect has enough to go on. Either there is no God, or God lacks the goodness or the power to save men. A hardened heart is unmoved by the tender solicitations of love. Therefore, when Jesus told his disciples to humble themselves and become like a child, he was warning them against hardness of heart. We do not experience hope by sheer accident. Hope is acquired by trust, trust by humility.

Some facts can be judged by a detached intellect, while some cannot. Detachment succeeds very well in astronomy or mathematics. But when the foundations of hope are considered, the convictions of the heart must join forces with the claims of the mind. And this implies more than a perfunctory association. A man must commit himself to the duties of love with a spirit of total dedication. This is the only way in which he will detect a connection between virtue and hope.

When a person is at home in the kingdom of love, the problem of evil is stripped of its terror. He joins those who are willing to let God explain himself at a time of his own choosing. As long as the heart is right before God, all else can be dealt with in a spirit of fellowship.

VIII

Martha and Mary may have known that Jesus received their summons. And they may have known that he intended to come to Bethany. But even though they had a stenographic report of Jesus' every word and action, they could never have discovered the precise reason why he chose to delay rather than come at once. He might have delayed for any number of reasons. Having been sent into the world by the Father, he was only free to do and say what the Father told him. Martha and Mary had no access to the intimacies of this sacred bond.

The sisters remembered something that skeptics tend to forget. They remembered that they were human beings. Human beings cannot probe the mind of God by asking themselves what they would do if they were God. They are men and not God. And if they are virtuous men, they will wait for God to reveal himself under conditions of his own choosing. To judge God in advance of this self-disclosure is manifestly wrong.

This left nothing but the vigil of waiting. And as Martha and Mary waited, they experienced a tingling sense of expectation. Although Jesus had disappointed them, this did not lessen their love for him. They knew that, after the time of waiting, Jesus would once again share the warmth of his life.

During this vigil the sisters may have reflected on the words of the prophet. "They who wait for the Lord shall renew their strength, they shall mount up with wings like eagles, they shall run and not be weary, they shall walk and not faint" (Isaiah 40:31). In any event, the sisters set a good example for all who know what it means to lose a loved one, and who are tempted to charge God foolishly as a result.

CHAPTER SIX

The Threat of Anxiety

"But, oh! this detestable tomorrow, a thing always expected, and never found."

— Samuel Johnson

When Jesus felt that the time had come to make his mission of mercy, he told the disciples to be on their way. "Then after this he said to the disciples, 'Let us go into Judea again'" (John 11:7). Bethany was about two miles from Jerusalem; it played an important part in Jesus' public ministry. It was here, in the house of Simon the leper, that Mary would anoint Jesus' feet with costly spikenard, and wipe them with her hair. From Bethany Jesus would set out on his triumphant journey to Jerusalem. Near Bethany the resurrected Lord would lift up holy hands and bless the disciples, then ascend to heaven.

Just now, however, the disciples were in no mood to visit Bethany. For when Jesus told them to follow him, they said, "Rabbi, the Jews were but now seeking to stone you, and are you going there again?" (v. 8). The disciples called Jesus Lord and Master. And yet when Jesus told them to follow him, they were ready to charge him with mistaken judgment.

The disciples were overtaken by a wave of anxiety, and anxiety is the father of fear. The disciples knew that by following Jesus to Judea they would endanger their own lives. Jesus knew this, too. And yet he chose to go right ahead with his plan. This is what disturbed the disciples. If a person *tries* to elude his pursuers, but is taken and killed despite all, he elicits pity. But if he purposely chooses to be taken, how can there be pity?

I

Jesus did not discuss the ethics of his plan. Instead, he told the disciples to redeem the time. "Jesus answered, 'Are there not twelve hours in the day? If any one walks in the day, he does not stumble, because he sees the light of the world. But if any one walks in the night, he stumbles, because the light is not in him' " (John 11:9). This might have struck the disciples as an evasion. But Jesus was not being evasive. Rather, he was showing his great love. He pitied the disciples, for he knew they could not accept the necessity of his sufferings and death. He remembered another occasion when he said that he must die at the hands of sinners. This word proved so disturbing that Peter volunteered to take Jesus' place. Peter was told to *follow* the Lord, not *correct* him.

Jesus delivered the disciples from the threat of anxiety, but he did it in a way they could not anticipate. Rather than trying to talk them out of their fears, he stirred up heroic impulses. When a person is given a chance to be a hero, his dignity is so perfectly accented that he overlooks the immediate threats to his life. So, Jesus said to the disciples, "Our friend Lazarus has fallen asleep, but I go to awaken him out of sleep" (John 11:11). When the disciples misunderstood the metaphor of sleep, Jesus told them plainly that Lazarus was dead.

The journey to Judea was now a moral obligation. "Nothing endears so much a friend as sorrow for his death," observes David Hume. "The pleasure of his company has not so powerful an influence."[1] If the disciples refused to pay their respects to Martha and Mary, they would pollute the very fountains of human dignity. Jesus gave the disciples a cause about which to rally; he taught them to save themselves by losing themselves.

The Lord's expedient contains a lesson for all of us. If we would be delivered from an excessive concern for ourselves, we must take time to be holy. As long as we are actively helping others, the venial effects of destructive anxiety can be detected and dealt with. And we actively help others by courtesy, consideration, and an outreaching spirit of forgiveness and understanding.

II

After Jesus relieved the threat of anxiety, he then went on to tell the disciples why he had purposely waited until Lazarus died. "Then Jesus told them plainly, 'Lazarus is dead; and for your sake I am glad that I was not there, so that you may believe. But let us go to him'" (John 11:14). Only Thomas spoke up. "Thomas, called the Twin, said to his fellow disciples, 'Let us also go, that we may die with him'" (v. 16). Thomas would go, though with a hint of resignation.

But was it not strange for Jesus to say he was *glad* he was not in Bethany when Lazarus became ill? Is this the language of love?

The strangeness disappears when we remember that Jesus was preparing for his final days on earth. He knew that the disciples would be severely tested by his sufferings and death. They would see him, the Lord of the new creation, end his ministry on a cross. Therefore, to preserve the disciples from feelings of despair, Jesus decided to give fresh proof that he was what he claimed to be, the very Son of God.

Hence, when Jesus offended Martha and Mary by failing to reach Bethany on time, he was purposely setting the stage for one of his mightiest miracles. This miracle would be such a

[1]Essay XXII, "Of Tragedy."

conclusive exhibition of divine power that the disciples would stay together during the dark hours between the crucifixion and the resurrection.

III

Destructive anxiety is a mysterious force.[2] It seems to take its rise out of the very capacities of freedom and self-transcendence that distinguish man from the brute. Whereas the brute finds selfhood in the world of nature, man is oriented toward eternity. Man can envision creative possibilities by projecting himself into the future. And once he does this, he is restless to improve the present. His vision provokes feelings of discontent, and discontent is the mother of progress.

God has ordained that man *should* exercise his capacities of freedom and self-transcendence. Just as a child takes pride in a finger painting, so his father takes pride in constructing a building or supervising an office. The fruits of creativity bear witness to man's dignity as a creature formed in the divine image.

But the difficulty is that man is born with self-centered affections. Rather than humbling himself before God, man asserts his own autonomy. Pride persuades him that security is found in power rather than love. And once pride succeeds in its mission, a concept of selfhood emerges which is loaded with all sorts of impossible standards of attainment.

Man invites destructive anxiety by undertaking a program of salvation for which he is not equipped. As he struggles to save himself, he finds that the future is full of threats as well as promises. His best laid plans can be frustrated by known or unknown forces; he must always be on guard. And in the end he must succumb to death. His symbols of power will fail him at last.

IV

Destructive anxiety has one certain sign: it leaves a person with undefined goals. Pride promises security through power,

[2]For what is possibly the profoundest study of anxiety, see Kierkegaard, *The Concept of Dread* (Princeton).

but pride fails to tell how *much* power is needed. Therefore, the self is left with a gnawing feeling of inadequacy. Power must be added to power, wealth to wealth, pretense to pretense. Otherwise a person is afraid that the base for selfhood is being eroded.

Since destructive anxiety cannot be subdued by the mere expedient of amassing power, an insecure person often tries to fend off despair by sustaining a pace which approximates perpetual motion. He believes that if he keeps moving, he will make progress toward selfhood. But his hope is based on an illusion, for progress is impossible unless we move between fixed points.

Many authors have described the futility of perpetual motion. But perhaps no author has described it with greater literary eloquence than Samuel Johnson. Sample: "The general remedy of those who are uneasy without knowing the cause, is change of place; they are willing to imagine that their pain is the consequence of some local inconvenience, and endeavour to fly from it, as children from their shadows; always hoping for some more satisfactory delight from every scent, and always returning home with disappointments and complaints."[3]

Possibly Johnson's most excellent passage is found in the section of the *Rasselas* where the purpose of a pyramid is being discussed. "It seems to have been erected only in compliance with that hunger of imagination, which preys incessantly upon life, and must be always appeased by some employment. Those who have already all that they can enjoy, must enlarge their desires. He that has built for use, till use is supplied, must begin to build for vanity, and extend his plan to the utmost power of human performance, that he may not be soon reduced to form another wish. I consider this mighty structure, as a monument to the insufficiency of human enjoyments. A king, whose power is unlimited, and whose treasures surmount all real and imaginary wants, is compelled to solace, by the erection

3*The Rambler,* No. 6.

of a pyramid, the satiety of dominion and tastelessness of pleasures, and to amuse the tediousness of declining life, by seeing thousands labouring without end, and one stone, for no purpose, laid upon another. Whoever thou art, that, not content with a moderate condition, imaginest happiness in royal magnificence, and dreamest that command or riches can feed the appetite of novelty, with perpetual gratifications, survey the pyramids, and confess thy folly!"[4]

The threat of destructive anxiety cannot be defeated by an endless round of diversions. Either time, strength, or interest will fail. Then boredom will set in, and boredom will render life vapid and uninteresting.

If boredom prompts a person to scrutinize the error of his way, it can be a beneficial experience. But generally it is the gateway to either a wasted life or despair. A proud person has relied on power for so long that he finds it difficult to believe he has missed the way. Boredom often drives a person to alcohol.

Alcohol restores a sense of adequacy, but it does this by disengaging man from reality. Troubles are dissipated by a lighthearted feeling of gaiety.

But the benefits of alcohol soon wear off. Then a person must either deal with his folly, or he must increase his drinking. To deal with folly is admittedly difficult, but it is not so difficult as dealing with the problem of compulsive drinking. An alcoholic surrenders both his self-control and his power to evaluate evidences.

V

It is ironic, but Alcoholics Anonymous has discovered a healing process which has affinities with that of the gospel. An alcoholic cannot be helped unless he returns to the kingdom of love. He must acknowledge that his power drives have gotten out of hand. Unless these drives are bridled, an alcoholic will continue to entertain such impossible concepts of selfhood that

[4]Chapter XXXII.

he will never get off the bottle. He will keep drinking to sustain a feeling of adequacy.

If power drives are to be brought under control, an alcoholic must be willing to become anonymous. He must withdraw from the competitive race for office, wealth, and authority. The weapon of Alcoholics Anonymous is full and complete humility. An alcoholic must want to quit drinking; he must admit that he can't quit; he must make an honest confession of faults; he must resolve to help others; and he must seek and accept the ever-present help of God. By being of service to others, the alcoholic renews his citizenship in the kingdom of love. He once again feels needed and wanted. He does not have to prove himself by displays of power. God then gives him grace to be the kind of a person that he could not be in his own strength.

All of this is friendly with one of the basic principles of healing in Christianity. Jesus says that we should humble ourselves and become like a child. A child can live a simple and contented life, for pride has not yet deceived him into thinking that life equals power. A child is content to be anonymous, as it were. He has a very modest concept of selfhood. Rather than striving to be a Hollywood celebrity or a corporation executive, he is busy making mud pies in the back yard.

Jesus, I am sure, would praise Alcoholics Anonymous for its wonderful work in leading men back to the kingdom of love. God abases the proud, but he gives grace to the humble.

Still, there is much more to selfhood than deliverance from alcohol. This is why Jesus did not dwell on the virtue of anonymity. He gave his life in order that he might lead many sons into glory. He knew that apart from the hope of eternal life, man is defenseless against the threats of destructive anxiety. If death ends all, man is doomed to futility.

VI

Alcoholics are not the only ones who must bridle power impulses. Pride does its best to convince all of us that life equals power. And when pride has its way, we imagine that we can complete our lives without submitting to the limits that God has written into the creation.

Jesus appealed to these limits when he reminded his followers that they were men and not God. "And which of you by being anxious can add a cubit to his span of life? If then you are not able to do as small a thing as that, why are you anxious about the rest?" (Luke 12:25-26). Man's attempt to save himself is as impossible as it is irrational. It would be easier to blot out the sun than to resist the limits that God has written into the creation.

Jesus says that man should learn, once and for all, that the task of salvation has been undertaken by God himself. When man forgets this, he loads his concept of selfhood with such ambitious standards of achievement that he becomes prey to destructive anxiety. He worries about what others think of him. He must keep up a front at all times.

Submitting to divine sovereignty does not imply human inactivity. Rather, it implies a willingness to distinguish between the things that belong to man and the things that belong to God. There is a time when we should *exert* ourselves, and a time when we should *submit* ourselves. For example, a farmer has no right to expect a good crop unless he prepares the soil and plants the seed. But after he has done everything he can, he must rest in Providence. He has no final control over the elements. If he frets about things that belong to God, he exposes himself to destructive anxiety. When such anxiety gets out of hand, it can create feelings of panic in the heart. These feelings can become so dreadful that a person will try almost any expedient for relief, even suicide.

We must train ourselves to rely on God for even the smallest benefits — our food, clothing, and shelter. If God did not dispense daily gifts, we would perish.

Jesus knew that if we would learn to rest in the sovereignty of God, the resulting sense of peace would deliver us from an excessive concern for material things. We would again realize that man's life does not consist in the abundance of his goods.

"Therefore I tell you," said Jesus, "do not be anxious about your life, what you shall eat or what you shall drink, nor about your body, what you shall put on. Is not life more than food, and the body more than clothing?" (Matthew 6:25). Life is another name for happiness, and happiness is only enjoyed when we are at peace with God. A man on the verge of suicide may *exist*; but he certainly does not *live*. He does not live, for he has nothing to live for. The flame of hope has flickered and died.

When Jesus advanced proof that God cares for man, he pointed to the manner in which God cares for the less valuable parts of creation. "Look at the birds of the air: they neither sow nor reap nor gather into barns, and yet your heavenly Father feeds them. Are you not of much more value than they?" (v. 26). Each time we see a flower in bloom or hear a bird in song, we are witnessing living proof that God is good.

VII

As Jesus and the disciples made their way toward Bethany, Martha and Mary continued their pious vigil. From time to time they may have asked if there was any sign of Jesus. There was none. At last the word came that Jesus and the disciples were drawing near. This was enough for Martha. She drew her wits about her and went out to meet the Lord. Being forward by nature, she welcomed the change of pace.

On another occasion Mary sat at the feet of Jesus, while Martha served. This order was now reversed. Martha was the student, while Mary remained in the house, a prisoner of grief. What was an advantage under one set of conditions proved to be a disadvantage under another. Let us learn a lesson from this. We must be careful neither to boast nor to despair. Wisdom will wait on God.

The longer Mary was left to herself, the greater was her feeling of insecurity. Brooding is always perilous, for it opens the door to anxiety. The intellect becomes clouded by emotion, and soon the heart imagines that the base for selfhood is being attacked.

The Lord knew that Mary would have difficulty saving face. So, he released her from the chains of grief by sending for her. Martha "went and called her sister Mary, saying quietly, 'The Teacher is here and is calling for you'" (John 11:28). Martha's quiet manners may suggest that Jesus had warned her against chiding Mary.

Jesus did not make an issue out of Mary's delay, nor did he let Martha gloat. He had one concern, and that was to give reassuring signs that all was well. Friends are not tossed and turned by little things that erupt in the moment. Love is an abiding relationship; it "bears all things, believes all things, hopes all things, endures all things" (I Corinthians 13:7).

When Jesus gave gentle signs of love, he not only released the sisters from the fear that they had to prove themselves, but he rendered it unnecessary to give an immediate explanation for his own delay. When hearts are reunited, the joys of love are so pleasing that grievances are pushed to one side.

VIII

Although Martha and Mary were different in personality and temperament, they shared similar feelings of anxiety. For when they greeted the Lord, they both said the same thing, as if there had been a rehearsal. "Lord, if you had been here, my brother would not have died" (John 11:21, 32). But there had been no rehearsal. The sisters both felt that Jesus had let them down, and from this common feeling they experienced a common anxiety.

One important thing should be noted, however. The sisters were anxious because of their identity with Lazarus, and not because they were defying the limits that God has written into the creation. Thus a distinction must be made between *constructive* and *destructive* anxiety. Let us enlarge on this.

When Lazarus grew ill, he had to depend on Martha and Mary for his very life. This sense of dependence delivered the sisters from competitive striving. They felt needed and wanted; they experienced peace of heart.

But when Lazarus grew worse, the sisters suffered a kind of anxiety that can only be known by those who faithfully discharge the duties of love. Martha and Mary saw Lazarus look up with pitiful eyes. But there was nothing more that they could do. In desperation they sent for Jesus, fully believing that his great love would constrain him to come at once. When he delayed, new waves of anxiety rolled across the soul. The sisters were plagued by all sorts of questions. Had they sent for Jesus soon enough? Had they made their message urgent enough? Possibly one of them should have importuned Jesus in person. But it was too late now. Lazarus was dead.

Here we face a paradox. Although love *decreases* destructive anxiety, it may *increase* constructive anxiety. For example, a mother may rest in the sovereignty of God, but this does not shield her from worry when her son goes to war or when her husband falls into financial distress.

If we seek decisive evidence that not all anxiety is destructive, we find it in the person of Jesus. Although he knew no sin, he did suffer anxiety. And he suffered *because* he knew no sin. His suffering grew out of his love. He saw the multitudes as sheep without a shepherd; he wept over Jerusalem.

But Jesus' love for his Father occasioned the greatest anxiety. When he faced the prospect of dying on the cross, his suffering was so intense that his sweat was like great drops of blood falling to the ground. He was inwardly troubled on several occasions, but the outward symptoms of anxiety were most noticeable when he prayed in the Garden of Gethsemane. Here he projected himself into the moment when he would expire on the cross as the Saviour of the world. Since his death would satisfy God's justice as well as reveal God's love, his suffering would be penal rather than disciplinary. He would drink the cup of the second death. At the moment of the atonement the Father would (as it were) turn his eyes from the Son, for God cannot have fellowship with sin. Jesus would cry, "My God, my God, why hast thou forsaken me?" (Mark 15:34) .

Jesus anticipated this experience while he prayed in the Garden. The critical pain was not the physical suffering, severe though this was. The critical pain was the experience of being rejected on account of sin.

We err, therefore, not knowing the Scriptures, if we say that *all* anxiety is a sign that a person is guilty of resisting the limits that God has written into the creation. Jesus cordially submitted to these limits, and yet he suffered great anxiety.

Constructive anxiety builds up dignity and respect, for life has no happier moments than when we suffer for those we love. Even when Jesus cried out on the cross, he experienced no conflict between what he was and what he ought to be. Only sin can create such a conflict, and Jesus was without sin.

IX

When Jesus finished his discourse on anxiety, he added a final note. "Therefore do not be anxious about tomorrow, for tomorrow will be anxious for itself. Let the day's own trouble be sufficient for the day" (Matthew 6:34) . This is a remarkable note, for it points up the *involuntary* elements in anxiety. Jesus knew that Martha and Mary were not anxious because they were guilty of thinking more highly of themselves than they ought. Their anxiety could not be helped; it grew out of the duties of love. Moreover, Jesus knew that many of his followers would experience elements of destructive anxiety, even though they did their best to rest in the sovereignty of God. In this case the anxiety would arise out of centers in the psyche that could not be named. We are fearfully and wonderfully made.

But if anxiety will plague us until the day of our death, how can we cope with it? In answer, Jesus says that partial deliverance can be found by channelling anxiety. If we *must* be anxious, there is enough trouble in the course of each day to occupy us. Destructive anxiety cannot defeat us unless it gets out of hand. And we prevent this by directing our concerns toward the troubles of the day. We must keep our anxieties manageable, as it were. "This present day has trouble enough attending it, we need not *accumulate* burdens by *anticipating* our trouble, nor borrow perplexities from tomorrow's evils to add to those of this day. It is uncertain what tomorrow's evils may be, but whatever they be, it is time enough to take thought about them when they come. What a folly it is to take that trouble upon ourselves this day by care and fear, which belongs to another day, and will be never the lighter when it comes? Let us not pull that upon ourselves all together at once, which Providence has wisely ordained to be borne by parcels. The conclusion of this whole matter then is, that it is the will and command of the Lord Jesus, that his disciples should not be their own tormentors, nor make their passage through this world more dark and unpleasant, by their apprehensions of trouble, than God has made it, by the troubles themselves. By our daily prayers we may procure strength to bear us up under daily troubles, and to arm us against the temptations that attend them, and then let none of these things move us."[5]

When we worry about things that are yet to come, we imply that *future* trouble, not *present* trouble, is the real threat to our security. We imagine that we are able to save ourselves in the present. But this is only another way of saying that we can dispense with divine sovereignty until anxiety gets out of hand.

To arouse us out of moral slumber, Jesus would have us reckon with the great number of troubles that lie all about us. And when we do this, we shall see that we are no more secure in the moment than we are when we face the future. Unless God is our *present* help, we are undone. "The universe at large would suffer as little, in its splendour and variety, by the destruction of our planet, as the verdure and sublime magnitude of a forest would suffer by the fall of a single leaf. The leaf quivers on the branch which supports it. It lies at the

[5]Matthew Henry, *A Commentary on the Holy Bible,* Matthew 6:34.

mercy of the slightest accident. A breath of wind tears it from its stem, and it lights on the stream of water which passes underneath.... We differ from the leaf only in this circumstance, that it would require the operation of greater elements to destroy us. But these elements exist. The fire which rages within, may lift its devouring energy to the surface of our planet, and transform it into one wide and wasting volcano. The sudden formation of elastic matter in the bowels of the earth — and it lies within the agency of known substances to accomplish this — may explode it into fragments. The exhalation of noxious air from below, may impart a virulence to the air that is around us; it may effect the delicate proportion of its ingredients; and the whole of animated nature may wither and die under the malignity of a tainted atmosphere. A blazing comet may cross this fated planet in its orbit, and realize all the terrors which superstition has conceived of it. We cannot anticipate with precision the consequences of an event which every astronomer must know to lie within the limits of chance and probability."[6] In addition to this we must add the great host of fortuities and accidents that stalk the streets of a complex social order. We are not safe, not for a moment.

When we realize that we are subject to troubles on all sides, we can understand why it is just as necessary to trust God for present mercies as it is to trust him for everlasting life. Nothing but an imaginary line separates the infinity of the past from the infinity of the future.

Once we cultivate the habit of trusting God in the present, the future will take care of itself; for the future cannot touch our lives until it is fragmented into present moments. And we *know* that God cares for us right now, for we are still alive and the planet on which we live is still intact. Present security is an earnest of future security.

[6]Thomas Chalmers, *A Series of Discourses on the Christian Revelation Viewed in Connection with the Modern Astronomy*, pp. 50-51.

X

As a final ideal for Christians, the Apostle Paul says that we should not let anything worry us. "Have no anxiety about anything, but in everything by prayer and supplication with thanksgiving let your requests be made known to God. And the peace of God, which passes all understanding, will keep your hearts and your minds in Christ Jesus" (Philippians 4:6-7). We make progress toward this ideal by training ourselves to rest in the sovereignty of God. God will either deliver us from troubles, or he will give us grace to bear them. In either case he will communicate steady assurances that our lives are precious in his sight. These assurances will serve as a dike against the forces of destructive anxiety.

Thus, when we are tempted to think that we are defenseless against the infinite troubles of the future, and that we cannot cope with the burdens of existence, we should remind ourselves that the present and the future are both alike to God. He says to future troubles, as he says to the tides of the sea, "Thus far shall you go, and no farther."

XI

One final observation must be made, however. Since Christians are saved sinners, and not restored angels, they are never wholly delivered from the temptation to think that they can complete their lives through power. This is why they should look on anxiety as a deadly killer. Hundreds of thousands of people are committed to mental hospitals each year, and many of them are Christians. As the pace of life increases, the incidence of emotional sickness will increase also. Christians may do their best to rest in the sovereignty of God, but in the competitive stress of modern living they may become more anxious about power than they ought.

That is not all. Since Christians are confronted by the law of God, they may invite psychic distress out of their very effort to live up to the terms of this law. The more they see imperfection in themselves, the more vulnerable they become to guilt feelings.

The psyche will accept a certain amount of repression. But when too many feelings are repressed, the psyche will take vengeance on the self by releasing its indigestible elements on the nervous system. Emotional illness may result. For example, a Christian may be distressed because he cannot overcome the habit of masturbation. He struggles and struggles, only to end defeated and guilty. If he does not learn to rest in the imputed righteousness of Christ, he may lose himself by trying to save himself. In this case he illustrates the paradoxical way in which *constructive* anxiety — anxiety suffered because the soul loves God — can open the sluice gate for *destructive* anxiety. Religious zealots often end up as neurotics. They fail to be as patient with themselves as God is.

Moreover, the local church can serve as a neurosis-producing agency by substituting legalistic attitudes for the freedom of grace in Christ Jesus. In this case the church becomes a cult which tries to play the role of the Holy Spirit by monitoring lives. The ethic of honesty is impaired, and believers are forced to repress their true feelings. Prolonged repression can damage both the emotions and the nervous system.

If anxiety reaches the place where we become victims of compulsive conduct, we should seek the help of a psychiatrist. Christians must be reminded of this, for in submitting to treatment they may think they are confessing that God has failed them. They should remember that they are struggling with *unconscious* forces. Whenever compulsive conduct is diagnosed as illness, Christians should rest in this diagnosis. Jesus would no more prejudice the rights of psychotherapy than he would the rights of medicine. There is a time and a place for everything. God brings healing through many agencies.

CHAPTER SEVEN

The Hope of the Resurrection

"Every man desires to live long, but no man would be old."
— Swift

Martha expressed her disappointment over Jesus' delay, but he made nothing of it. Instead, he disclosed a truth that caused her ears to tingle. "Jesus said to her, 'I am the resurrection and the life; he who believes in me, though he die, yet shall he live, and whoever lives and believes in me shall never die' " (John 11:25). These words have brought more comfort to more sorrowing Christians than any other in Scripture, except the Twenty-third Psalm and the fourteenth chapter of John. Without the hope of the resurrection we could not be certain that the kingdom of heaven fulfills and completes the kingdom of love.

I

Martha was a receptive student because she kept her wits about her. Grief, we know, can exercise strange powers. It can unfit a person for calm reflection and steady action. For example, a physician may tell his patient that he is suffering from a

94

serious disease, and that he must submit to major surgery — only to see his patient cast himself on the irresponsible claims of a charlatan.

Bereaved people are especially vulnerable, for they are bound by the duties of love. They want to do all they can to prove their devotion to the departed. Therefore, unless a mortician is a man of character, he may corrupt his trade by encouraging the bereaved to buy an excessively expensive funeral. He is guilty of not doing as he would be done by.

A detached intellect sometimes takes a sophisticated attitude toward funeral ceremonies. Why spend money on a coffin and flowers? Everything that can be done for the dead has already been done. And after all, what *is* a corpse, but a mass of chemical elements?

No upright person can take a detached attitude toward death, for the body of the departed forms part of the image that love retains. This is why a mortician is encouraged to make the corpse appear as lifelike as possible. Memories acquired during the funeral service must last a long time; for when the bereaved looks back on the beloved, he pictures the beloved in the state of serenity created by the mortician.

The decomposition of the body may be accepted as a scientific fact, but this fact is defied whenever the bereaved places flowers on the grave. The image of serenity is retained long after worms have done their destructive work. When a mother visits the grave of her child, she conducts herself as if the little one were actually watching her. Fellowship between kindred minds does not terminate at death.

Call it folly, call it wishful thinking: the fact remains that no upright person can believe that his loved ones are only animals that perish. The intellect may accept the gloom of the grave, but the intellect is not authorized to speak for the heart. The heart draws on convictions that are foolishness to both science and philosophy. An upright person knows that if the departed do not count, then the living do not count, for the living and the departed are inseparably joined by the bond of love.

The cemetery may be located in one of the most prominent parks in town; our files may house the latest life-expectancy statistics; and we may compose a definitive textbook on the decomposition of the body. But the accumulated force of this evidence cannot void the convictions of the heart. The hope of eternal life forms the very foundation of the kingdom of love, for love is an eternal tie.

When a person shifts to the mood of detachment, of course, he can easily believe that death ends all. For example, he says he has no difficulty seeing himself in a coffin. He can accept his own nonexistence without a whimper. But in this rather macabre experiment he forgets one important thing: he forgets that the person in the coffin is not himself at all. It is a figment of the imagination, for he himself is a spectator, very much alive, and very much in possession of personal dignity.

When we approach the question of death with our heart as well as our mind, we can no longer remain detached. We realize that we are judging the very meaning of existence itself. This is why we are shocked when we hear that a friend has been snatched away by death. His death challenges our assumption that we live by right as well as by fortune. It awakens us to the fact that the relation between the kingdom of love and the kingdom of heaven is not an academic matter which we can probe at our convenience.

The more we suffer in the cause of love, the more our heart assures us that the kingdom of love forms the outer court of the kingdom of heaven. We believe that our departed loved ones are somewhere, that is all. They count in the eyes of God, even if they do not count in the eyes of man. Both the funeral service and the final burial place are enlisted as supports of this hope. The departed are said to rest in peace until that dawning day when hearts will again be united and all tears dried,

II

When Jesus told Martha that Lazarus would live again, she readily believed. "Martha said to him, 'I know that he will rise again at the resurrection at the last day' " (John 11:24). Martha was part of a believing community. This community looked to God, not to man, for the final defeat of evil in history. The resurrection of the body was proof of this defeat.

In the early chapters of Semitic history the hope of the resurrection was veiled behind the symbol of Sheol. Job was one of the first to protest against the gloom of the grave. The heart cries out for higher things.

As Israel's sense of national destiny developed, pious Jews began to look for a kingdom in which God would rule over his people in perfect peace and justice. The hope of the resurrection was eventually associated with the establishment of this kingdom, for how else could God gather his people together, that they might dwell with him forever? "Thy dead shall live, their bodies shall rise. O dwellers in the dust, awake and sing for joy! For thy dew is a dew of light, and on the land of the shades thou wilt let it fall" (Isaiah 26:19).

When the Jews passed through the bloody Maccabean period, many of the faithful laid down their lives as martyrs. At this time the Semitic sense of justice joined with the promise that God would bless those who put their trust in him. That which had been spoken by Daniel was now more fully understood: "And many of those who sleep in the dust of the earth shall awake, some to everlasting life, and some to shame and everlasting contempt" (12:2). If God lets his people suffer martyrdom, how much more will he vindicate them before their enemies? And how can such vindication take place, unless there is a resurrection of both the just and the unjust?

Jesus accepted this teaching. He said that a correct view of God implies a correct view of the resurrection. "But that the dead are raised, even Moses showed, in the passage about the bush, where he calls the Lord the God of Abraham and the God of Isaac and the God of Jacob. Now he is not the God of

97

the dead, but of the living; for all live to him" (Luke 20:37-38). God would not be a blessing to his people unless he raised them from the dead, for man is body as well as soul.

Since Martha remained a child at heart, she had no difficulty believing that God would reunite families after the shock of death. Her heart assured her that good people have nothing to fear, now or at any other time. God had already shown his love toward Israel through centuries of covenantal history. The blessings of the covenant and the convictions of the heart met in the hope of the resurrection.

III

Martha confessed her faith in the resurrection of the body, but Jesus was not content to leave the matter there. He went on to explain how the kingdom of heaven would be ushered in. He himself, in his very person, enjoyed authority over death. He was the resurrection and the life. He received this authority from the Father as a fruit of covenantal obedience. And in accordance with this authority, he would see that the kingdom of heaven fulfilled and completed the kingdom of love. All who passed their days in the fear of God would be clothed with heavenly bodies.

When Jesus finished this happy disclosure, he asked Martha, "Do you believe this?" To which she replied, "Yes, Lord; I believe that you are the Christ, the Son of God, he who is coming into the world" (John 11:27). Martha was not sure *how* Christ would exercise his Messianic office. But she was sure of one thing, and that was enough. She was sure that Christ was uniquely related to God. "And even now I know that whatever you ask from God, God will give you" (v. 22). Jesus proved his divinity in many ways. The lame walked, lepers were cleansed, the dead were raised up, and the poor had good news preached to them. Hence, Martha was convinced that if Jesus asked the Father to raise the dead, the Father would do what he asked. And since Jesus loved Lazarus, he would surely see that Lazarus was given a resurrection body.

The doctrine of the Trinity is a stumbling block to Jews, for it seems to offend the Semitic confession that God is one. And it is altogether likely that Martha herself, had she been pressed, would have confessed that she did not know precisely how Jesus was related to the Father. But Jesus did not burden her with matters that would be clarified when the apostles drew up the theology of the church. It was enough that Martha was willing to take Jesus at his word. She could not go beyond that, even *with* the fullness of apostolic revelation.

IV

Jesus relieved Martha's fears, though he did it in a way that she did not expect. Rather than explaining why he did not reach Bethany before Lazarus died, he directed her thoughts to the hope of the resurrection. With this hope established, nothing else was of great importance. This means that Jesus consoled Martha without directly solving the problem of evil. He not only failed to explain why he had been tardy, but he made no effort to explain why God was pleased to create a world into which such frightful things as sickness and death would enter.

How, then, did Jesus deliver Martha from an excessive concern for the problem of evil? The answer is, he satisfied the convictions of the heart. Since Martha humbled herself like a child, she placed no more demands upon Jesus than a child would. When a child follows the conflict between good and evil in a fairy tale, he does not become anxious until it appears that good people are being defeated. As long as good people live happily ever after, the convictions of the heart are satisfied.

Since Martha lived by a wisdom that God dispenses to all who humble themselves, she was not shattered by the problem of evil. Her heart raised one question: Do good people count, or do they not? And when Jesus assured her that Lazarus would rise again, the question was answered. The kingdom of heaven *would* fulfill and complete the kingdom of love. All else could be borne in patience.

Jesus gave no hint that Martha would see Lazarus before the

general resurrection, and it did not occur to Martha to ask Jesus to exercise his Messianic powers then and there. She was too meek to pressure the Lord. As far as she could tell, the general resurrection might not take place for thousands of years. Not only would she pass her days visiting the grave of Lazarus, but within a time all too short both she and her sister would walk through the valley of the shadow of death. Still, she believed. And she believed with an assurance that could not be challenged by the problem of evil. Since the Lord *promised* to gather his friends into the kingdom of heaven, what more could be asked?

When Martha said she believed that Jesus was the resurrection and the life, she was actually making a twofold confession. She was confessing, first, that Jesus had power to raise the dead; and second, that when and how he exercised this power were matters that he alone, in fellowship with the Father, could decide. Martha knew that the secret things belong to God, while the revealed things belong to us and to our children. Jesus might have left Bethany without making the slightest effort to restore Lazarus. And if he had chosen this course, Martha would have cheerfully submitted. In doing so, she would have set a good example for all who are tempted to think that God is tardy in fulfilling his promises.

V

When the Apostle Paul preached in Athens, his audience listened until he spoke of the resurrection. "Now when they heard of the resurrection of the dead, some mocked; but others said, 'We will hear you again about this'" (Acts 17:32). It is ironic that the Greeks were offended by the very doctrine that evokes the highest feelings of joy in Christians. Paul was so certain of his ground that he linked the very hope of mankind to the resurrection of Christ. "Now if Christ is preached as raised from the dead, how can some of you say that there is no resurrection of the dead? But if there is no resurrection of the dead, then Christ has not been raised; if Christ has not been raised, then our preaching is in vain and your faith is in vain" (I Corinthians 15:12-14). Christ's resurrection is proof that the Father received the sacrifice of the Son. All who are in Christ will be raised in like manner, for Christ is the first fruits from the dead.

The Greeks wanted eternal life, but they saw little point to the resurrection of the body. Since the real man is the rational man, the body is an extraneous element. And even worse, it is a positive hindrance to man's unclouded vision of truth. We are saved by being divested of body, not by being reunited to body. Socrates drank the hemlock on the confidence that he would soon be liberated from his corporeal prison.

Plato is very eloquent when he tells of the pleasures that the soul will enjoy when it is no longer encumbered by a body. "It has been proved to us by experience that if we would have pure knowledge of anything we must be quit of the body — the soul in herself must behold things in themselves: and then we shall attain the wisdom which we desire, and of which we say that we are lovers; not while we live, but after death; for if while in company with the body, the soul cannot have pure knowledge, one of two things follows — either knowledge is not to be attained at all, or, if at all, after death. For then, and not until then, the soul will be parted from the body and exist in herself alone. In this present life, I reckon that we make the nearest approach to knowledge when we have the least possible intercourse or communion with the body, and are not surfeited with the bodily nature, but keep ourselves pure until the hour when God himself is pleased to release us. And thus having got rid of the foolishness of the body we shall be pure and hold converse with the pure, and know of ourselves, the clear light everywhere, which is no other than the light of truth."[1] As Plato saw matters, a resurrection body would only extend man's present miseries into the life that is to come.

Martha rested in the Semitic conviction that man is a vital

[1]*Phaedo,* 66-67.

union of body and soul. If you take away the body, you take away an essential part of man. This is why the hope of eternal life was eventually linked with the hope of the resurrection.

The Semites not only enjoyed the light of special revelation, but they came at the issue by way of the convictions of the heart. Thus, when Martha tried to picture Lazarus in the kingdom of heaven, she could only picture him as she knew him in Bethany. If he did not have a body like unto the one that she remembered, he would not be the same person.

A child would say that Martha was right. How can a person live happily ever after, unless he has a body that makes him the person he is, and not somebody else?

Since Martha could not conceive of Lazarus apart from body and soul (what would he possibly look like?), her faith in the resurrection was as natural as her faith in the sovereignty of God. The Greeks were content to believe that only the intellectual part of man survives the shock of death. They reached this conclusion because they divorced the claims of mind from the convictions of the heart. They spoke from the perspective of detachment.

The hope of the Greeks would strike a child as rather odd. Of what value would the intellect be unless we have a body through which to express it? And how could unclothed intellects have any fun? Moreover, it would be drafty.

If Jesus had been on hand, he might have told the Greeks to imitate the manners of a happy child. Through this exercise they would apprehend truths that remain concealed to a detached intellect. And chief among these truths would be the connection between hope and the resurrection of the body. When a child thinks of his grandfather, he thinks of the only grandfather he knew: the one with a peculiar gait and a certain smile, the one with rough hands and large ears. If God gives grandfather a *better* body than he had on earth, that is quite all right. But the child knows that if his grandfather has no body at all, he is no longer a human being; and if his body is not like the one he had on earth, no one would recognize him.

VI

Since all observable evidence supports the conclusion that man perishes at death, the resurrection of the body is as offensive to science as it is to philosophy. And when Christians speak of a *spiritual* body, critics say that the end of good sense has come.

But the Apostle Paul thought otherwise. In fact, he went to considerable pains to tell just what the resurrection body would be like. It would belong to a new order of physics. "What is sown is perishable, what is raised is imperishable. It is sown in dishonor, it is raised in glory. It is sown in weakness, it is raised in power. It is sown a physical body, it is raised a spiritual body" (I Corinthians 15:42-43). But how did Paul expect cultured people to believe this? The answer is, he told them to behold the risen Lord. Jesus was raised from the dead, and his body was spiritual in substance. He not only ate fish with his disciples, but he passed through closed doors. Therefore, as Paul saw the issue, Jesus' resurrection body proved that God not only *could* create a new order of physics, but that he actually *did*. Reality itself sets the limits to possibility.

Paul was fully convinced that Jesus was raised from the dead. The evidences were sufficient, for Jesus "appeared to Cephas, then to the twelve. Then he appeared to more than five hundred brethren at one time, most of whom are still alive, though some have fallen asleep. Then he appeared to James, then to all the apostles. Last of all, as to one untimely born, he appeared also to me" (vv. 5-8).

The Greeks groaned under the limitations that sin places on our present bodies. This is why they wanted to be emancipated. They knew that the body is subject to passions which war against the soul.

But since the Greeks did not have the light of special revelation, they did not know that the resurrection body will be divested of sin. When man is confirmed in righteousness, the conflict between soul and body will cease. The body will become a servant of the soul.

The Prophet Haggai speaks of the coming Messiah as the desire of all nations. This prophecy symbolizes the wider biblical teaching that the gospel of Jesus Christ is congenial with the noblest aspirations of the human heart. All upright men long for a society that will be characterized by perfect peace and justice. Jesus has guaranteed this society by his resurrection from the dead. Hence, his resurrection "is not an arbitrary and violent fact, standing in sharp contradiction to the spiritual, which are the true regnant, forces of the universe; nor is it an irrational unconnected event, whose only right to be believed is that it happened. It is the sublime symbol, perhaps rather prophetic realization, of truths which the colder intellect of the world has doubted and criticized, fearing they were too good to be true, but which its warmer heart has everywhere victoriously striven to believe. Man is not born to die, and death, though universal, has not quenched his belief in his own immortal being. There is no fact of human experience so remarkable, so significant of the power of the reason to command, to conquer, and to defy the senses. The intelligible world is created from within, not from without; what man believes he believes in obedience to the laws of mind, often in rigorous opposition to the alien and inhuman forces of matter. And this is nowhere so vividly seen as when he stands throughout all the centuries of his history daring, in the very face of death, to believe in his own continued being. An experience as old and as universal as the race has not been able to compel the reason to regard the grave as its end, or physical dissolution as meaning annihilation of spirit."[2] Common and special grace meet in the person of Christ.

VII

When the Apostle Paul made his defense before King Agrippa, he raised a question that every child would consider perfectly in order. "Why is it thought incredible by any of you that God raises the dead?" (Acts 26:8). If God created man to

2A. M. Fairbairn, *Studies in the Life of Christ*, p. 334.

enjoy the kingdom of love, why can't he recreate him to enjoy the kingdom of heaven? God is sovereign; he does the whole counsel of his will. As far as a child is concerned, a puppy is proof that God is sovereign, for who but God could have created a puppy?

The resurrection of the body is a great mystery, of course, but this does not disturb the heart of a child. A child knows that unless God helps good people, they will be overwhelmed in the end. This is why fairy tales leave room for miraculous intervention. If miracles are needed to ensure the final triumph of goodness, so be it. In this case, miracles are as much a part of reality as trees and rivers.

A child knows that it is much more difficult to accept the defeat of goodness than it is to accept the reality of miracles. If good people do not live happily ever after, then what difference does anything else make? The most important thing has been surrendered. Death has triumphed over life.

A child keeps values in their proper order because he judges ultimate issues in and through the convictions of the heart. He believes that good people will be guided safely from the kingdom of love to the kingdom of heaven. And when good people gather together in heaven, they will enjoy a vital union of body and soul. *Angels* can get along without bodies, but human beings cannot.

Jesus says that a child is right. And to prove his point, he invites his friends to draw near and inspect his own resurrection body. "And he said to them, 'Why are you troubled, and why do questionings rise in your hearts? See my hands and my feet, that it is I myself; handle me, and see; for a spirit has not flesh and bones as you see that I have'" (Luke 24:38-40). The resurrected Lord is living proof that God is able to raise the dead. This settles the issue for a child, and it also settles it for all who humble themselves and become like a child. Would Jesus deceive his friends?

CHAPTER EIGHT

The Tears of Jesus

"All clannishness is divisive."

— Kierkegaard

Mary answered Jesus' call, but she was too choked with grief to say much. After expressing her disappointment over his delay, she burst into tears. And there was power in her tears. The mourners felt this power, and so did Jesus. "When Jesus saw her weeping, and the Jews who came with her also weeping, he was deeply moved in spirit and troubled" (John 11:33).

When Jesus first learned that Lazarus was ill, he told his disciples he was glad he was not there. Jesus knew how Mary's tears would affect his human nature. Only by being absent could he wait on the fullness of time. That fullness had now come.

Jesus asked to see where Lazarus was buried. As far as the mourners could tell, he only wanted to pay his last respects to the dead. They said to him, "Lord, come and see" (v. 34). It was here that the fountains of sorrow were broken up. "Jesus wept" (v. 35).

I

Mary's tears had power, but Jesus' tears had greater power; for when the mourners saw Jesus weeping for Lazarus, they were constrained to say, "See how he loved him!" (v. 36). And once they said this, they went on to confess that Jesus enjoyed Messianic powers. "Could not he who opened the eyes of the blind man have kept this man from dying?" (v. 37). A hush fell over the group as the Holy Spirit worked freely.

It is ironic, however, that Jesus' tears symbolize one of the reasons why Christians in later ages have been divided in theology. Weeping seems to overturn the historic confession that Jesus is truly God as well as truly man. How can Jesus be truly God, when tears trace to emotions, and emotions to bodily change? God has no body; he is without parts and passions.

The historic confession is patterned after the biblical teaching that Jesus united humanity to his deity at the moment of the incarnation. "In the beginning was the Word and the Word was with God, and the Word was God. . . . And the Word became flesh and dwelt among us, full of grace and truth" (John 1:1, 14).

The elements in this teaching seem clear enough. And indeed they are. Yet, the conservative branch of the church has often been so anxious to defend the Lord's divinity that it has slighted the Lord's humanity. The result has been a stern, implacable Mediator who bears little resemblance to the man who wept at the grave of Lazarus.

Determined to correct this picture, the liberal branch of the church has gone in quest of the historical Jesus: the Jesus who hungered and thirsted, who did not know the hour of his own return, and who was a man of sorrows and acquainted with grief. Since the liberals reminded the church that Jesus was touched with the feeling of our infirmities, they performed a needed service.

But many liberals were not content with this. They pressed their quest until they found a person who was only human and not divine. But recent biblical scholarship (form criticism, for example) has shown that the liberal Christology was founded on the sands of insufficient evidence. Scripture speaks of only one Jesus: the divine Son of God who assumed humanity at the moment of his incarnation. Jesus' tears witness to his humanity, while his authority to forgive sins witnesses to his divinity. Only man can weep, only God can absolve.

We may not be able to explain how Jesus unites two centers of consciousness and will in one person. But this inability does not authorize us to postulate a Messiah whose psychology we *can* explain. Christ is a gift of revelation, and revelation is enveloped in mystery.

Liberals do not relieve the difficulty by saying that the historical Jesus can be found in a stratum of the New Testament that is more primitive, and thus nearer the oral traditions, than the strata which develop the concept of the God-Man. Precise scholarship knows that a single, self-consistent view of Christ is found in the New Testament. No matter which part of revelation is considered most primitive, that part represents Jesus as a person who simultaneously expressed divine and human attributes. Jesus stilled the waves, cured congenital blindness, and accepted worship. Yet, he became weary from his journey, paused for refreshment, and by prayer and intercession sought daily strength from his heavenly Father.

This is what Scripture teaches. And nothing will be gained by trying to go beyond this teaching, for everything we know about the nature of Christ is found in Scripture.

II

Martha was not offended by the fact that Jesus expressed divine attributes. On the contrary, she knew that apart from these attributes he would not be able to save good people from the grave. Martha accepted Jesus in the totality of his person. He not only spoke as one having authority, but his actions corresponded to his words. Jesus came to Bethany for rest, yet even the demons obeyed him.

Martha symbolizes the high standard of faith set by women

in the New Testament. "It was no wonder that the hearts of women were drawn to such a Saviour in the days of His earthly life. When we think how the quick intuitions of womanhood in moral and spiritual things, its swift instinctive recognition of truth and purity, holiness and love, when embodied in living character, often far outstrip the colder reasonings and conclusions of men, we shall easily understand how the best and purest of the daughters of Israel were among the first to see, or rather to feel in their inmost souls, the glory of Christ, and to receive Him as their Lord and Saviour.... The evangelists tell us of no woman who ever came to Christ and went back from Him again, of none who betrayed or denied her Saviour, of none even who in any special manner forsook Him at the end."[1]

Martha did not know how Jesus united divine and human attributes. But she was sure that he did, for her senses did not deceive her. We often experience more than we understand. For example, we *know* what pain is, but we cannot *tell* what it is.

A believer may pass his entire life without being able to satisfy his mind that Jesus unites divine and human attributes. But competence in theology is never cited as a requisite for salvation. Jesus saves us by grace alone. Our sole responsibility is to be good.

A believer may be compared to the blind man who knew that Jesus healed him, but who could not give a precise account of what happened. "The poor man was ignorant of the author of his cure; he knew not the sacredness of His Person, the offices which He sustained, or the errand which brought Him among men. Much ignorance of Jesus may remain in hearts which yet feel the power of His blood. We must not hastily condemn men for lack of knowledge; but where we can see the faith which saves the soul, we must believe that salvation has been bestowed. The Holy Spirit makes men penitents long before he

---

[1]D. Douglas Bannerman, *The Scripture Doctrine of the Church* (Eerdmans), p. 314.

makes them divines; and he who believes what he knows shall soon know more clearly what he believes."[2]

When Jesus asks us to believe on the testimony of his own word, he does what a good man anywhere would do. For example, if a child finds it hard to believe that there are sound waves which a radio can hear but which people cannot, his father does not overwhelm him with technical data. The child is told to wait until he gets to college. In the meantime he should believe that there *are* such sound waves, and he should believe because his father says there are.

III

When the mourners gathered at the grave of Lazarus, they experienced perfect unity. Jesus himself was the rallying point for fellowship, doctrine, and form: *fellowship* because the mourners were bound by cords of love; *doctrine* because the teaching of the Lord was normative; and *form* because the will of the Lord became the will of the group. The mourners were all of one mind.

The church remained united after Jesus ascended to heaven and questions of doctrine and form had to be settled by the apostolic college. These questions did not disrupt the unity because they were placed at the service of the fellowship. The believers knew that if they failed to love one another, their profession in doctrine and form would profit nothing.

When great numbers were added to the church, this ideal was not surrendered. The believers were together in the temple; they were together from house to house.

It was not long, however, before believers began to boast that they were of Paul, Apollos, and Cephas. Party spirit corrupted the purity of the fellowship. The tragedy of a divided church is almost as old as the joy of a united church. Party spirit has plagued the fellowship from the middle of the apostolic age until now. The verdict of history is clear.

[2]Charles Spurgeon, *Morning and Evening Daily Devotions* (Zondervan), p. 139. Used by permission.

IV

The Roman Catholic Church played a leading role in guiding believers from the warmth of Pentecost to a time when believers not only faced the wrath of the empire and a spawn of heresies, but when they could look neither to Jerusalem as the center of worship nor to the collective wisdom of the living apostles. A magnificent effort was put forth, and with many lasting benefits.

But at least one capital mistake was made. The Roman Church began to crystallize its traditions before the epistles of Paul had been thoroughly circulated and studied.[3] As a result, the full import of justification by faith was not comprehended. A Roman believer could never rest in the finished work of Christ; he could lose his salvation at any time by committing a mortal sin. A spirit of legalism sullied the biblical concept of grace. This spirit did much to obscure the fellowship, for love and fear are moral opposites.

When the Roman Church faced the spawn of heresies, it was so anxious to preserve internal unity that it lodged the *charisma veritatis* in the bishop, rather than in the original apostolic college. The church was then conceived as the continued incarnation of Christ. Christ was present in the person of ecclesiastical officers.

With the triumph of form, the Roman bishops dealt harshly with prophets who tried to call the church back to the teachings of the original apostolic college. Rome believed then, as it does now, that no man is rightly joined to Christ unless he is rightly joined to his bishop. This means that justification is decided by a believer's relation to an institution, rather than by personal confrontation with Christ.

Luther repented of sin; he received Jesus as Lord and Saviour; and he believed all that was spoken by the prophets and apostles. But these virtues fell short of Roman requirements.

[3]See Thomas F. Torrance, *The Doctrine of Grace in the Apostolic Fathers* (Eerdmans).

An offense against the form of the church was the same as an offense against fellowship and doctrine.

Rather than gently correcting Luther, Rome excommunicated him. The great schism in Western Christendom traces as much to Roman intransigence as it does to Luther's own sense of individualism. No real opportunity was given to investigate the relation between fellowship, doctrine, and form.

When Luther and his congregation sang *A Mighty Fortress Is Our God,* one of the great moments in the life of the church was realized. Luther succeeded in liberating the fellowship from the confines of form. And by this liberation he opened the way for the purifying of doctrine.

V

In an alarmingly short time, however, Lutheranism converted to an institution which defined faith as assent to right doctrine, and which granted the prince many of the rights enjoyed by the Roman bishop. Lutherans were no more charitable to dissenters than Roman Catholics were. An Anabaptist could repent of sin; he could receive Jesus as Lord and Saviour; and he could believe all that was spoken by the prophets and apostles. But these virtues fell short of Lutheran requirements. Unless a penitent affirmed, according to the Wittenberg Concord, "that with the bread and wine are truly and substantially present, offered, and received the body and blood of Christ," he was not part of the fellowship.

The intestine struggles in Lutheranism, together with the historic tendency of Lutherans to go it alone, can only be accounted for on the assumption that doctrine and form rank higher than fellowship.

The disturbing part of Lutheran particularity is the fact that insufficient allowance is made for either the subtle scholastic arguments that undergird the Lutheran view of the eucharist, or for the inability of believers in other traditions to feel the force of such arguments.

112

VI

Calvin performed the spectacular feat of delivering the church from state control.[4] His penetration of divine grace left little place for human complacency. The *Institutes* forms the finest treatise in Protestant theology. Aesthetic proportion and personal piety blend with a scholar's command of Scripture.

But when Calvinism converted to a theological system, it turned out that the "elect of God" were those who accepted the distinctive teachings of John Calvin. Once again, doctrine and form ranked higher than fellowship. An Arminian could repent of sin; he could receive Jesus as Lord and Saviour; and he could believe all that was spoken by the prophets and apostles. But these virtues fell short of Calvinistic requirements. Unless a believer accepted the doctrine of irresistible grace, he was not part of the fellowship.

Calvinism did not create an institution as such, but it imitated Catholicism and Lutheranism by drawing up a confession that would serve as a touchstone of correct doctrine, and thus of fit fellowship. But this confession, like those it imitated, was never ratified by the church universal.

Calvinism had no excuse for freezing theological inquiry at the level of the *Institutes*. A careful examination of that document will show that Calvin himself, despite his great genius, failed to harmonize the divine decrees with human responsibility. Now, if a theology is defective at such a critical point, how can it serve as a norm of fellowship?

VII

The British fear of innovation insulated Anglicanism from the more radical by-products of the Reformation. Gradually a way was opened for high, medium, and low expressions of liturgy within the one church form.

Outsiders may think that Anglicanism has reverted to the age of the Judges, where each man does what is right in his

[4]See Emil Brunner, *The Misunderstanding of the Church* (Westminster).

own eyes. But more discriminating minds will perceive that Anglicanism is a majestic, if not altogether unique, effort to subordinate form to fellowship. An Englishman is not much of a gentleman if he is dishonest, and especially when he worships God. Decent decorum requires, therefore, that full allowance be made for the differences in temperament that exist within the various strata of society. By this expedient, greater liberty in the Spirit is encouraged. Some Christians prefer a minimum of ritual, while others feel impoverished unless the ritual is ancient and elaborate.

But the British fear of innovation has all too often been federated with a subtle defense of British interests. Although Anglicanism defends the church universal in its articles of faith, in the real business of daily life it reserves patronage and power for Anglicans.

The religious wars in England trace, in great part, to the intransigence of the established church. Dissenters could repent of sin; they could receive Jesus as Lord and Saviour; and they could believe all that was spoken by the prophets and apostles. But these virtues fell short of Anglican requirements. Unless a believer supported the traditions of the established church, he was not part of the fellowship.

VIII

When the Puritans, Scotch Presbyterians, and Methodists succeeded in overturning the papacy, the crown, and the established church, the Christian community was given fresh opportunities to make the fellowship as wide as Christ intended it. But each group was too occupied with improving its own position to take creative leadership in this higher question.

The Puritans restored the classical standards in theology. They composed a body of literature which was a credit to that or any other day. No major topic in the theological encyclopedia was left unexplored.

But the Puritans (with notable exceptions) tended to be parochial in outlook, for they never succeeded in transcending the limitations of Calvinism. They used the distinctive elements in this theology as a measure of correct doctrine, and thus of fit fellowship. They envisioned a theocracy reserved for the "elect."

Scotch Presbyterians drank the full cup of Reformation heroism. They followed Knox in putting their feet on the necks of kings and queens, while bowing in the dust before Almighty God.

But Scotch Presbyterians impaired the fellowship by insisting that presbyterian polity was the only biblical polity. Once again, fit fellowship was decided by correct doctrine and form. Moreover, Scotch Presbyterians, like many Lutherans, have tended to link the interests of the church with the interests of race and soil.

Methodists successfully rebuked Anglican formalism by returning to the biblical emphasis on personal holiness. Although Methodism did little to advance the dialogue in classical theology, it did write an inspiring chapter in frontier evangelism. The gospel was preached with unexampled power and conviction. A lively hope was brought to the working classes.

But many Methodists were not satisfied with this. They used the doctrine of personal holiness as a denominational status symbol, and thus as a reason for separating from the church universal. And when Methodists resisted this cultic tendency, they imitated Anglicanism by drawing up an episcopal polity which reserves patronage and power for Methodists. And since Methodist polity is untempered by the British symbols of the crown and the British gift of understatement, it is often more rigid and bureaucratic than Anglicanism.

IX

Baptists and Congregationalists have hit the trail of independence. They say that the New Testament refers to the local congregation as a church. The evidence is not conclusive, of course, but it is sufficient to encourage the conviction that every local congregation is a self-contained unit. All other associations are voluntary expedients aimed at encouraging richer fellowship between congregations. The Bible is elevated above human creeds, and each believer enjoys liberty of conscience as a priest of God.

With this catalogue of virtues to draw on, independent churches ought to enjoy ideal conditions for the improvement of Christian fellowship. But there is often a wide gap between theory and practice.

The woes of Baptists and Congregationalists are easy to recount. As life in the communion becomes more involved, there is a gradual encroachment upon the liberty of the local congregation. The "voluntary associations" eventually assume the form of an institution. In the end, loyalty to Christ is equated with loyalty to the denomination. It is ironic, therefore, that local Baptist and Congregational churches often have less liberty than congregations under the parish system.[5]

X

The separatist settles things by organizing a church of which he himself is the head. His policies are crudely dictatorial, yet he sometimes encourages levels of fellowship which the historic denominations frown on. The diversity of spiritual gifts is accepted without embarrassment, and a genuine effort is made to encourage lay participation.

But the way of the separatist is seldom a happy one. Being out of fellowship with both the church universal and the wisdom of the ages, the separatist is prey to novelty and enthusiasm. He cannot discern shades of better and worse in his own theology; he has no biblical answer to anarchy. Moreover, he is inflated with a feeling of personal superiority. Rather than trying to heal existing divisions in the church, he is busy creating new ones.

[5]Paul M. Harrison says it is high time that Baptists develop a genuine representational system of government. See *Authority and Power in the Free Church Tradition* (Princeton).

XI

Many believers in the modern church are searching for a happier way to blend fellowship, doctrine, and form. They are gathering for friendly, exploratory conversation. This is a genuinely hopeful sign.

Still, the effort only points up the paradox of our witness as Christians. Individual believers may be willing to surrender institutional status, but the institution itself, with its vested interests and tangled bureaucracy, goes right on defending the status quo. In one room there is conversation about enlarging the fellowship, while down the hall committees are busy devising new ways to perpetuate the patronage and power of the institution.

What can be done about this paradox? Well, for one thing we can *acknowledge* the paradox. Since the church falls short of the ideals set down in Scripture, we might just as well come right out and admit it.[6] Nothing will be gained by either wringing our hands in despair, or by dreaming of utopian conditions that overlook the limits that original sin places on history. With all our lofty theories of the church, the grim fact remains that the institution is more concerned with jurisdiction than it is with fellowship. Money must be handled and property titled. As vested interests evolve, new power blocs are formed to protect them.

If the church were to acknowledge its imperfection, a climate of honesty might be created in which believers could wait on the Holy Spirit to show them happier ways to blend fellowship, doctrine, and form.

XII

There is little reason to believe that the denominations will ever succeed in drawing up a confession that is acceptable to all parties. Confessions not only mirror the times, but they have a disturbing way of converting to final, inspired docu-

[6]See Lesslie Newbigin, *The Household of God* (Friendship Press).

ments. If a theologian proposes that a confession be brought into more perfect harmony with Scripture, he is charged with departing from the faith once for all delivered to the saints.

The Roman Catholic Church forthrightly announces that its confessions are infallible. But this only adds to the paradox of our witness as Christians. When Rome summoned the Council of Trent in the pressure of the Counter Reformation, it not only acted with haste, but it drew up a creed that was defined against the excesses of sixteenth-century Lutheranism. But how can Rome improve upon a creed that has been declared infallible?

XIII

The modern church is trying to shrink the paradox by merging denominations of like heritage. Such mergers, when undertaken with proper ends in view, should by all means be encouraged. If Christians agree on doctrine, they should learn to agree on form. Denominational reduplication not only hinders the fellowship, but it is an inexcusable waste of money and talent.

But merger is not the whole answer. For one thing, it may serve as a substitute for individual responsibility. Shrinking the number of denominations is no blessing *per se*. Christ prayed for unity, but not for organizational unity. He prayed that his followers might be one, even as the Father and the Son are one. This implies a *vital* unity, and vital unity implies fellowship. Thus, if organizational merger detracts Christians from their obligation to love one another, it is a hindrance to unity, not an encouragement.

Moreover, the major denominations grew out of a sincere effort to honor the teachings of Scripture. Scripture does not claim to give a finished system. When the Apostle Paul says, "I know in part," he speaks for the whole church.

It is only natural, therefore, that theologians will disagree on questions such as polity, the eucharist, the subjects and modes of baptism, predestination, and degrees of sanctification. And such disagreements are bound to be reflected in the forms which the Christian community assumes when it enters history. We should not be ashamed of our theological differences. They are signs that we are taking the work of exegesis seriously. Furthermore, a genuine Christian fellowship can exist *within* the framework of denominational plurality. Love can hurdle existing barriers.

Roman Catholicism insists that it is the only true church, but its claims are refuted by the plain facts of history. Whether Rome cares to acknowledge it or not, God has true believers in *every* professing church. All we can do is stand back and rejoice at the manifold operations of divine grace. Whenever there are genuine signs of faith and repentance, we must presume that the gospel is at work. And having made this admission, we then should try to find some way to bring all Christians into fellowship.

Roman Catholicism is in an awkward position. Whenever it says it is willing to hold conversation with "separated brethren," it simultaneously affirms and denies that there is no salvation outside the church.

XIV

Despairing of a confessional route to unity, many are proposing that we unite around a least common denominator. This denominator will be so all-inclusive that no believer will be excluded from the fellowship.

The expedient is attractive, but it has its price. Once we become indifferent to right doctrine, it will not be long before we shall also become indifferent to fit fellowship; for the two go together. Saving faith does not take place in a vacuum. It is an act that grows out of a vital response to the gospel, and the gospel is based on specific redemptive events. If we disparage these events, we surrender the normative elements in the Christian religion.

XV

Many obstacles stand in the way of Christian brotherhood. But if we sincerely believe in the communion of the saints, we must continue to strive for more perfect ways to express this brotherhood in history. If God has ordained that doctrine and form should be servants of the fellowship, then we should see that God's will is done on earth as it is in heaven. Whatever impedes the fellowship must be brought under critical scrutiny.

Some help may be found by returning to the grave of Lazarus. When Jesus wept, the mourners were so perfectly controlled by the Holy Spirit that they were delivered from any temptation to seek status in power rather than love. If we were more affectionately united with the tears of Jesus, we might be less anxious to exclude believers who do not agree with us in the details of doctrine and form.

The first evidence that we have been touched by Jesus' tears is an acknowledgment that *love* is the sign of a true disciple. Jesus says, "By this all men will know that you are my disciples, if you have love for one another" (John 13:35). If we fail to radiate the love of God in our lives, our achievements in doctrine and form will profit nothing. This is taught in Scripture with such force and clarity that only hardness of heart could miss it. "If I have prophetic powers, and understand all mysteries and all knowledge, and if I have all faith, so as to remove mountains, but have not love, I am nothing. If I give away all I have, and if I deliver my body to be burned, but have not love, I gain nothing" (I Corinthians 13:2-3). Love crosses over denominational lines. It puts itself in another's place; it does as it would be done by.

When believers make a sincere effort to enter into each other's lives, they will not only give local expression to the unity for which Christ prayed, but they will be in a better position to extend this unity beyond themselves. They will appreciate why Christians in other traditions believe as they do. And when the warmth of these traditions is felt, believers will be less tempted to think that they enjoy exclusive access to grace and truth.

If the denominations are serious in their desire to liberate the fellowship from the confines of doctrine and form, they should take immediate steps to encourage interdenominational conversation. This can be done in many creative ways: by exchanging pulpits and seminary lectureships, by arranging programs of personal visitation, and by the use of literature from other denominations. Every pastor should do his part to create a climate in which signs of fellowship are honored wherever they are found and under whatever conditions. And above all, status should be given to the prophet who stimulates a healthy discontent by reminding the church that form and doctrine are servants of the fellowship, and not the other way around.

Christians find their identity by personal confrontation with Christ. And the proof of this confrontation is not assent to doctrine, and certainly not membership in an institution. The proof is a gentle, outgoing charity that takes in all men, and especially those of the household of faith.

Surely it behooves the church to dedicate its energies to an adorning of the one virtue that makes man most like his Maker, and Christians most like their Lord.

If Christians would learn to love one another, the day might come when they would be willing to pray with one another, and perhaps even to confess their faults to one another. In that happy day the eyes of the understanding would be opened to see that the scandal of Christendom is not the plurality of denominations, but the manner in which believers seek status in doctrine and form, rather than love.

CHAPTER NINE

The Queen of Christian Virtues

"Nor love thy life, nor hate; but what thou liv'st
Live well; how long or short permit to Heaven."
— Milton

When Jesus asked Martha if she believed that he was the resurrection and the life, she made a good confession. *Certainly* she believed; she believed with all her heart; she would let the whole world know where she stood.

Within a few moments, however, Martha's conduct belied her confession. For when Jesus drew near the tomb of Lazarus — again, deeply moved in spirit — he asked that the tomb be unsealed. Martha was displeased by this, and she came right out and said so. "Lord, by this time there will be an odor, for he has been dead four days" (John 11:39). The disciples tried to hinder Jesus from going to Bethany, while Martha tried to hinder him after he arrived.

Jesus was a mystery to his own generation. His mother chided him for tarrying in Jerusalem at the age of twelve. His disciples rejected the necessity of his sufferings and death. And the

122

temple officers were resentful at his common upbringing, his residence in Galilee, his poverty, his choice of friends, his view of the kingdom, and above all his attitude toward the traditions of the elders.

I

Why was Martha displeased when Jesus asked that the tomb of Lazarus be unsealed? Well, for one thing, she may have thought that he was being inconsiderate. If he had put himself in her place (so she may have reasoned), he would have realized that her vanity would be wounded by the unveiling of a corpse. Martha was the anxious hostess. And if she was disturbed by dust under the table or by a gnat in the wine, how much more would she be disturbed by the odor of death, and that of her own brother?

Since Martha's conduct belied her confession, Jesus rebuked her mildly but firmly. "Did I not tell you that if you would believe you would see the glory of God?" (John 11:40). Jesus said, as it were, "Martha, you have just confessed that I am the resurrection and the life. Now you must learn to live by your confession."

Jesus was gentle, for he knew that Martha meant well. It was possible, so far as her conscious intentions were concerned, that she thought she was acting out of a regard for the Lord's own welfare. She may have wanted to spare him an experience that she would want to be spared, had she been in his place. He was near the tomb, where the odor of death would be strongest.

Martha's conduct illustrates the risks of love. For when Martha tried to do as she would be done by, she did not make sufficient allowance for the temperamental difference between male and female. Since *she* would be revolted by the odor of death, she presumed that Jesus would, too. She did not appreciate the degree to which the average male can be objective about putridity. A little girl may scream when she sees a dead snake at her feet, while a little boy may tuck the snake in his pocket as a real prize.

Only love can deal with the risks of love. When good people

misunderstand one another, they clear the air by friendly conversation. Each new disclosure makes it easier for love to do as it would be done by.

II

If Martha's faith had been strong, she would have rested in the will of the Lord, even though the Lord was not doing what *she* would have done, had she been in his place. Possibly this is why Jesus did not explain his mission. He may have been teaching Martha a lesson in faith. And by teaching her, he would be teaching all who would come in his name thereafter. Faith is strong when it takes pleasure in what the Lord says or does, and for no other reason than that the Lord says or does it.

Scripture speaks of "heroes of the faith." Certain believers earned this title because they continued to rest in the promises of God, though things about them seemed to go against these promises. Judged by daily experience, the heroes had good reason for wondering if God had forsaken them. They "were stoned, they were sawn in two, they were killed by the sword; they went about in skins of sheep and goats, destitute, afflicted, ill-treated" (Hebrews 11:37).

But how did the heroes keep on believing? Did they surrender their critical faculties? The answer is, they focused their attention on the only evidence that really mattered. Since God had *promised* that he would build a city with foundations, the issue was settled.

If Martha's own faith had been heroic in quality, she would have rejoiced in whatever Jesus chose to do. She would have reminded herself that since Jesus was uniquely related to God, the very wisdom of God flowed through him.

God does not expect us to comprehend the relation between Providence and history. But he *does* expect us to trust him. "And without faith it is impossible to please him. For whoever would draw near to God must believe that he exists and that he rewards those who seek him" (Hebrews 11:6).

When a believer learns to trust God, he has an antidote for daily suffering. Each time he suffers, he reminds himself that the kingdom of heaven completes and fulfills the kingdom of love. The suffering then becomes an exercise in discipleship. Strong faith knows that when God has given his word, the case is closed.

III

Since Martha acted from good motives, it follows that her *faith,* not her *love,* was on trial. This is an important distinction. While love implies a steady sharing of natures, faith may rise or fall, depending upon the sufficiency of the evidences, or at least upon the mind's ability to detect this sufficiency. Martha experienced a conflict between her heart and her mind. In her heart she dearly loved the Lord, though in her mind she wondered if he was doing as he would be done by. She questioned the Lord's wisdom, but not the Lord's integrity.

Martha's conduct proves that faith can be upset by things to which love pays no attention. Martha was not alone in this. Even Abraham, the father of the faithful, experienced a conflict between his heart and his mind. When God promised him a son, Abraham found the promise so intellectually unacceptable that he laughed. But his laughter was a sign of weak faith, not imperfect love. His mind merely rebelled against the idea that an old man could have a son. Such things simply don't happen; they are unscientific.

In due time, however, Abraham's faith reached the level of his love, for God gave him the very son whose coming had been doubted. Abraham learned an important lesson from this. He learned that once God has given his word, a believer should train himself to rest in that word. Heroic faith is not disturbed when it detects a seeming discord between what God has promised and what is actually taking place. With God all things are possible.

After Abraham's faith rose to the level of his love, he believed God with such steadfastness that he became a model for future generations. When God told him to offer up Isaac — the son whom he loved — he instinctively obeyed. He believed that God was able to raise Isaac from the dead.

Jesus detected signs of weak faith in his disciples, but he did not love them any less on that account. Having put himself in their place, he knew why they found it hard to accept his sufferings and death. Love is a vital sharing of natures. It is not a legal contract.

The disciples continued to follow the Lord (Judas excepted), even though their faith at times was weak. Their love triumphed over their faith. When they were disturbed by something that Jesus did, they came right out and said so. Since Jesus loved them, they knew he would not use the truth against them, not even the truth that they were disturbed by what he was doing.

On some occasions Jesus strengthened faith by adding the force of external evidence. For example, when he appeared in his resurrection body, he did more than *say* he was the Lord. He invited his bewildered disciples to come and touch him. In this way he helped subdue the forces of involuntary unbelief. The disciples *wanted* to believe, but they found it *hard* to believe. The Evangelist Luke says that the disciples "disbelieved for joy" (24:41). The struggle between heart and mind could hardly be expressed more perfectly.

Scripture names love as the queen of Christian virtues. "So faith, hope, love abide, these three; but the greatest of these is love" (I Corinthians 13:13). Faith is the instrumental cause of justification, but only love can define man's self-giving possibilities as a creature made in the image of God.

Jesus named love as the sign of a true disciple. He then went on to say that a disciple would in no way distinguish himself above Gentiles and tax collectors unless he loved his enemies and prayed for those who persecuted him.

But how can a disciple love his enemies? Isn't this a contradiction in terms? Enmity implies a separation, not a vital sharing, of natures.

The answer is, "love" and "like" are not synonyms. Love is a much more comprehensive term; it connotes every conceivable degree of sympathy, pity, and understanding. Thus, we can *love* a person, even though we do not *like* him, for love can exist

126

where there is no affection. Scripture states the attributes of love in such a manner that all possible relationships of life with life are anticipated. "Love is patient and kind. Love is not jealous or boastful; it is not arrogant or rude. Love does not insist on its own way; it is not irritable or resentful; it does not rejoice at wrong, but rejoices in the right" (I Corinthians 13:4-6).

In other words, when we *like* a person, we have a natural affection for him. But a Christian does not have to wait until he experiences natural affection. He simply asks, "How would I want to be treated if I were in another person's place?" And since this question can be raised under all possible conditions — even when we stand in the presence of our enemies — a Christian is never exempt from the royal law. To love our enemies means to do as we would be done by.

IV

Long after the event, Martha may have wondered why she tried to prevent Jesus from unsealing the tomb of Lazarus. In the course of such an inquiry she may have found that sin creates confusion in the heart of a believer. In other words, she may have found that her actions and her desires were at war with one another. Her impulse to challenge the Lord erupted out of areas in the psyche that she could not identify. In her heart of hearts she wanted to be an obedient disciple. But when Jesus asked that the tomb of Lazarus be unsealed, something happened inside her. Even though she wanted to believe that Jesus was doing the right thing, she impulsively rushed forward. She did the very thing she did not want to do, though at the time she thought that it *was* what she wanted to do. In her devotional self she cheerfully confessed that Jesus was Lord; but in her historical self she failed to live by what she confessed.

The Apostle Paul conducted a normative inquiry into this problem, and when he finished he found that a believer is host to two conflicting laws: the law of the mind and the law of sin. This is why a believer suffers a gap between what he is and what he ought to be. Paul realized that his historical self did not carry out the ideals set down by the devotional self. "I do not understand my own actions. For I do not do what I want, but I do the very thing I hate" (Romans 7:15).

We can easily imagine the sort of actions to which Paul referred. Perhaps he retired to his chamber after a strenuous preaching mission, only to experience an eruption of impatience when a late knock was heard at the door. But how did this square with Paul's teaching that love is patient and kind? Again, he may have muttered silent profanities when he pricked his finger while working on tents. But how did this square with his teaching that the heart must be pure before God?

Paul could have been discouraged, for he was too honest to deny the conflict between the law of the mind and the law of sin, and too virtuous to pretend that the conflict was innocent. Then how did he continue to enjoy peace of mind?

The answer is, he reversed the field by viewing the conflict through the eyes of mercy and grace. Paul knew that God accepts us through faith and repentance, not through works of righteousness done in the flesh. If God were to judge believers by their conduct in the historical self, they would be lost and undone. Believers are accepted because they are clothed with the righteousness of Christ.

In other words, Paul saw that the real issue was not the law of sin as such, but the moral attitude that a believer takes toward this law. God has created us as we are; we cannot undo the creation. But there is something we *can* do: we can choose to be good. And one way we do this is by siding with the law of the mind against the law of sin. In this way we prove that our dominant affections are holy.

We may say, in broadest terms, that a regenerate man wants to be good, but evil gets in the way; while an unregenerate man wants to be evil, but good gets in the way. Both men suffer a conflict, though the position of the dominant affections is reversed in each case. A regenerate man *despises* the law of sin, while an unregenerate man does not.

Since Paul longed to be better, he proved that he cordially submitted to the law of God. "Now if I do what I do not want, I agree that the law is good" (Romans 7:16). But if this is the case, why did Paul fail to carry out the ideals set down by his devotional self? The answer is, his historical self was partly controlled by affections that traced to the law of sin. "For I delight in the law of God, in my inmost self, but I see in my members another law at war with the law of my mind and making me captive to the law of sin which dwells in my members" (vv. 22-23). Paul *wanted* to live a more perfect life, but his historical self lacked the needed power. The spirit was willing but the flesh was weak.

In other words, Paul interpreted the conflict from within justification by faith. Since he *hated* his lack of perfection, he proved that his dominant affections were regenerated; and in this he rejoiced. He knew that a hatred of imperfection is one form of perfection. "Thanks be to God through Jesus Christ our Lord! So then, I of myself serve the law of God with my mind, but with my flesh I serve the law of sin" (v. 25).

Paul also knew that the conflict between the law of sin and the law of the mind would continue until God redeems us from our unregenerate bodies. "We know that the whole creation has been groaning in travail together until now; and not only the creation, but we ourselves, who have the first fruits of the Spirit, groan inwardly as we wait for adoption as sons, the redemption of our bodies" (Romans 8:22-23).

V

The Pauline construction will offend moralists who do not understand that gracious relationships are judged by love and not law. Friends have little use for the nice distinctions of a legal code. They are joined by cords of love, and love seeks nothing but evidences of love. These evidences can be given in one of two ways: either by spontaneously doing what is right, or by expressing spontaneous sorrow for having failed. We may call this the principle of double fulfillment.[1] The principle never holds in *legal* relationships, but it always holds in *gracious* relationships. As long as channels of fellowship are kept open, good people do not allow signs of legal imperfection to impede the progress of love. The imperfection may actually reveal the degree to which a friend is being tyrannized by the law of sin in his members. If he hates his failures, he proves that his heart is right.

The principle of double fulfillment comprehends all gracious relationships. Take the average home, for example. The mother may at times be impatient and critical, the children thoughtless and inconsiderate. But these occasional faults do not rob love of its joys, for each member of the family sincerely wants to do better in the future. A confession of faults is conclusive proof that the heart is actively struggling against the law of sin.

The principle of double fulfillment can be illustrated by the charming candor of the child who, when rebuked for teasing baby brother, asks, "But Daddy, why do I *like* to tease baby brother?" The child knows that it is wrong to tease. And more than this, he wants to stop teasing. Yet, he has hardly finished his glass of milk when he looks for new opportunities to tease. A detached intellect would say that the child is being perverse, and ought to be punished. But love puts a different construction on the evidences. Since the child *wants* to be good, love says that his teasing traces in large part to the law of sin in his members. Perversity does not care if it hurts another person. The child does care.

Love knows that a person is good when he is kind and truthful. But love also knows that there are two ways in which goodness can be expressed: directly by being kind and truthful, or indirectly by expressing sorrow for failure. And indirect fulfillment is just as morally acceptable as direct fulfillment, for it is an evidence of love. Love does not make a capital issue out

[1]For a more detailed defense of this principle, see my work *Christian Commitment* (Macmillan).

of faults. After a husband asks his wife to forgive him, the case is closed.

Whenever we fail to take cognizance of the principle of double fulfillment, our attitude toward others becomes harsh and unfeeling. We surrender our gentle role as sinners saved by grace. "Nothing is more unjust, however common, than to charge with hypocrisy him that expresses zeal for those virtues which he neglects to practice: since he may be sincerely convinced of the advantages of conquering his passions, without having yet obtained the victory; as a man may be confident of the advantages of a voyage, or a journey, without having courage or industry to undertake it, and may honestly recommend to others those attempts which he neglects himself."[2]

When Jesus was asked if we should forgive a brother seven times, he replied that we should forgive him seventy times seven. In other words, we should forgive him as often as he seeks forgiveness. His contrition is proof that he is actively struggling against the law of sin in his members. We have no right to hinder this struggle.

VI

Now that the principle of double fulfillment has been explored, we can come to grips with a problem that has lurked in the shadows from the first moment we appealed to the convictions of the heart. These convictions say that a man is good when he is kind and truthful, and that in the end a good man has nothing to fear. But how does this square with Jesus' teaching that no man is good?

The answer is quite within reach, providing we look in the right place. When Jesus says that no man is good, he is judging the human race according to the strict demands of the divine law. This law says that a man shall love God with all his heart, and his neighbor as himself. Only Christ fulfilled the requirements of this law. Even his enemies could find no fault in him.

It was not necessary that his enemies be in possession of the written law of God; for the law is written on the heart as well

[2]Samuel Johnson, *The Rambler*, No. 14.

as in the Bible. "When Gentiles who have not the law do by nature what the law requires, they are a law to themselves, even though they do not have the law. They show that what the law requires is written on their hearts" (Romans 2:14-15). Just as the kingdom of heaven fulfills and completes the kingdom of love, so the law of God fulfills and completes the convictions of the heart. The law of God says that we should love. The convictions of the heart say the same thing, for to love *is* to be kind and truthful.

Since Jesus loved God with all his heart, and his neighbor as himself, he brought human nature to perfection. He witnessed to the very ideals that we honor in our devotional self, but which we offend in our historical self. His perfection is a judgment against our imperfection. We are kind and truthful some of the time, but not all of the time.

Hence, when Jesus says that no man is good, he is announcing how we stand when the convictions of the heart are used as a measure of legal righteousness. Judged by the absolute standards of kindness and truth, we are unprofitable servants. We *have* sinned and come short of the glory of God.

The gospel is the good news that God offers pardon to those who, when judged by the strict requirements of the law, are guilty. God only asks us to be honest in acknowledging our guilt. This honesty is not a base for personal merit, but it *is* an occasion for forgiveness. Christ created this occasion by taking the curse of the law upon himself. "For you know the grace of our Lord Jesus Christ, that though he was rich, yet for your sake he became poor, so that by his poverty you might become rich" (II Corinthians 8:9). God is willing to deal graciously with sinners, and in gracious relationships the principle of double fulfillment takes over. A believer is delivered from the fear of law.

When God calls on sinners to repent, he calls on them to receive the witness of his Son. This is what is meant by believing on Christ as Lord and Saviour. Believers not only acknowledge that the Lord brought human nature to perfection, but they accept this perfection as a judgment against their own imperfection. They then are graciously received by God.

If a person *says* he repents of sin, and yet refuses to accept Christ as Lord and Saviour, he has a faulty understanding of either the requirements of the law, the heinousness of his own transgressions, or the gracious character and Messianic office of Jesus Christ. He is inconsistent in the way he carries out his own moral philosophy.

When God forgives a sinner for Christ's sake, he does more than deliver the sinner from the just penalty of law. He brings him into a settled, filial relation by adopting him into the family of God. The sinner is henceforth treated as a child of God. "For all who are led by the Spirit of God are sons of God" (Romans 8:14). Legal imperfection has no bearing on the moral standing of a child, for the little one is received by love and not law.

Since a Christian is a child of God, he should not become discouraged when he discovers a gap between his devotional self and his historical self. Nor need he think that his standing before God is in jeopardy unless he brings some offering or bears some punishment in his body. Jesus says that whom the Son sets free, he sets free indeed. And he does this by assuring his friends that the Father seeks nothing but evidences of love. These evidences are formally the same as those that good people seek on any gracious level of life. A child of God either spontaneously does the will of God, or he expresses spontaneous sorrow for having failed. Regardless which course he takes, he proves that his dominant affections are at war with the law of sin. Nothing more is required.

For example, the Apostle Peter denied the Lord thrice. But this sin, though heinous in the sight of God and man, is given no special attention in the New Testament. And there is a valid reason for this silence. When Peter sinned, he went out and wept bitterly. His tears were evidence of contrition, and that ended the matter. When Jesus met Peter, he told him to feed God's sheep. Jesus knew that a memory of this sin could destroy Peter's effectiveness as an apostle. By creating a gentle atmosphere of fellowship, Jesus reminded Peter that *God himself* had dealt with the curse of the law. Peter was not to bring this curse upon himself. Or, as the Apostle Paul puts it, "For you did not receive the spirit of slavery to fall back into fear, but you have received the spirit of sonship" (Romans 8:15).

The conduct of children, when judged by the strict terms of law, is seldom free from condemnation. But this does not jeopardize their moral standing in the home. When children confess their faults, they are praised for taking an active stand against the law of sin.

VII

Since a detached intellect is blind to the manners of love, it raises what it thinks is a decisive objection to the principle of double fulfillment. It says that if a Christian can discharge his responsibility by the mere expedient of expressing sorrow for failure, then a Christian is armed with an excuse for perpetrating the worst kind of wickedness. Whenever he commits a crime, all he has to do is say he is sorry. He then can go on as if nothing had happened.

The Apostle Paul anticipated this objection when he asked if we should sin that grace may abound. The very thought was revolting, for how can love turn against its own essence? Since friends share each other's nature, they are fettered by cords of love. They have no peace until they are in fellowship with one another, and fellowship thrives on habits of kindness and truth. When friends hurt one another by unkindness and untruth, they experience a compulsion to make things right. This compulsion is part of the essence of love. Friends go to one another and seek forgiveness. They could give no more convincing proof of personal integrity.

So it is with our relationship with God. Since believers share in the divine nature, they hunger and thirst after righteousness. They would no more think of deliberately hurting God than they would of deliberately hurting a friend.

When a Christian confesses sin, therefore, he is not trying to evade the seriousness of sin. On the contrary, he makes his confession because he is constrained by a love of righteousness. He is seeking relief from the feeling of guilt that accompanies a rupture of fellowship. Since he shares his nature with God, he naturally wants to get right with God.

As soon as a Christian makes an evangelical confession, the blood of Jesus Christ cleanses him from all unrighteousness. The issue is carried no farther. There are no temporal punishments to be borne, no oppressive memories to be suffered. God "does not deal with us according to our sins, nor requite us according to our iniquities. For as the heavens are high above the earth, so great is his steadfast love toward those who fear him; as far as the east is from the west, so far does he remove our transgressions from us" (Psalm 103:10-12).

VIII

Jesus rebuked Martha for her lack of faith, but this was an act of discipline, not an act of penal affliction. Discipline is a family matter; it has no relation to a court of law. Jesus bore the curse of the law with the express purpose of leading many sons into glory. The law may reveal pollution in the heart of a believer, but it is no longer an instrument of condemnation. It cannot define a believer's relation to God. "There is therefore now no condemnation for those who are in Christ Jesus. For the law of the Spirit of life in Christ Jesus has set me free from the law of sin and death" (Romans 8:1-2).

Let us illustrate this from daily life. The presiding magistrate in a court of justice has to pass sentence on those who have broken the law. In the course of a day he may send many young men to jail. But if he returns home and finds that his own son has stolen money from family sources, he does not put on his judicial robes and call court into session. He is concerned with discipline, and discipline is a work of love. He takes whatever steps are best for the boy: a scolding, a spanking, or the removal of any number of privileges, with restitution. Or he may decide to do nothing at all. A good judge will be as merciful as the law allows, whereas a good father will be as merciful as love allows. The severity of the discipline is decided by the needs of the beloved. The same transgression may at one time be met with a slap on the wrist, and at another time by a mere glance of disapproval. Since discipline is aimed at helping the beloved in his struggle against the law of sin, love knows when to discipline and when not to discipline. It does as it would be done by.

If a Christian sins, it may be necessary for the Lord to discipline him. But the discipline is concerned with correction, not condemnation. "And have you forgotten the exhortation which addresses you as sons? — 'My son, do not regard lightly the discipline of the Lord, nor lose courage when you are punished by him. For the Lord disciplines him whom he loves, and chastises every son whom he receives.' It is for discipline that you have to endure. God is treating you as sons; for what son is there whom his father does not discipline?" (Hebrews 12:5-7). If we confuse correction with condemnation, we not only misrepresent Scripture, but we expose our hearts to the frightful prospect that God rejects us. We must be on guard against making such a mistake. "For it is the property and business of a tender father to correct his children, when disobedient; but of a Judge and of an executioner, to pronounce a person worthy of punishment and to inflict it, which, in the proper sense of *punishment,* makes no part of the Divine conduct toward the heirs of glory. When their heavenly Father chastises them, it is not merely to demonstrate his own sovereignty, but to correct for faults committed; and that not in wrath, but in love. Yea, he does it because he loves them, in order to make them partakers of his holiness, and that they may not be condemned with the world. This being the design of God in chastising his people, and the severest chastisements being a fruit of his paternal care; though the means be grievous, yet they are salutary, and the end is glorious."[3]

3Abraham Booth, *The Reign of Grace,* p. 213.

The logic of discipline may seem nebulous to outsiders, but not to those who honor the duties of love. Love knows what is best for the beloved, for it does as it would be done by.

If love does not have enough information to go on, it gains this information by engaging in friendly conversation. Love examines what should be examined; it overlooks what should be overlooked. But no matter what course it takes, it never creates a legal atmosphere in which the beloved is afraid that he will be rejected.

IX

Martha may have regretted the manner in which her actions belied her confession. But a memory of this incident did not depress her. She knew that her standing before the Lord was not decided by degrees of legal righteousness. As long as she was actively struggling against the law of sin in her members, she proved that her dominant affections were holy. And in gracious relationships this is all that matters.

In ourselves, apart from our mystical union with Christ, we have no ground for hope. Therefore, we live by faith in the Son of God who loved us and gave himself for us.

Believers make their calling and election sure by living open and sincere lives. They invite God to know them and try them. This willingness to submit to divine scrutiny is an evidence of love, and love seeks nothing but evidences of love.

CHAPTER TEN

These Things Were Not Done in a Corner

"The writers against religion, whilst they oppose every system, are wisely careful never to set up any of their own."

— Edmund Burke

The arrow of discipline found its mark, for Martha drew to one side, there to wait with Mary and the mourners. She did not wait long. In the space of a few moments Jesus performed a miracle whose power surpassed comprehension, whose blessing surpassed expectation. By the sheer word of his mouth, without secondary means, Jesus reversed the decree of death. "When he had said this, he cried with a loud voice, 'Lazarus, come out.' The dead man came out, his hands and feet bound with bandages, and his face wrapped with a cloth" (John 11:43). It is difficult for the mind to take in the immensity of this miracle. Lazarus was not only dead, but buried; not only buried, but subject to decay. There had been no collusion at the grave, for both Martha and Mary believed that the tragedy was beyond repair. Moreover, many mourners witnessed the scene, and they wept. Pious people are powerless to simulate tears.

I

It is important to note that Jesus ended his public ministry with the raising of Lazarus. "Jesus therefore no longer went about openly among the Jews, but went from there to the country near the wilderness, to a town called Ephraim; and there he stayed with the disciples" (v. 54). In the stillness of this setting Jesus began the instruction that reached its climax in the fellowship of the Last Supper.

Although the Lord was soon to return to the Father, he assured his disciples that they had nothing to fear. Not only would he send the Holy Spirit to be their comforter, but after the gospel had been preached to all nations, he himself would return in power and glory.

The reason why Jesus delayed his trip to Bethany was now abundantly clear, though as yet the disciples did not appreciate this reason. With the raising of Lazarus, Jesus gave incontrovertible proof that he was what he claimed to be, the Messiah of God. This proof would bring comfort to his friends, even as it would arouse resentment in his enemies. The comfort was intended, the resentment could not be helped.

Jesus knew how his disciples would feel when they would see him standing before a jeering multitude, mute and bowed, seemingly void of authority. By raising Lazarus from the dead, he gave conclusive evidence that he was uniquely related to God; for only God has power to create life.

Thus, no matter how sorely the disciples might be tested as they saw the Lord being tried and condemned, they would have no reason to despair, for they had optical assurance that he was the resurrection and the life.

II

The raising of Lazarus also served as a direct preparation for Jesus' triumphant entry into Jerusalem and the swiftly moving events that led to his trial and crucifixion. The stupendous nature of this miracle caused a sharp cleavage in Israel. A decision for or against Christ had to be made; neutrality was no longer possible. "Many of the Jews therefore, who had come with Mary and had seen what he did, believed in him, but some of them went to the Pharisees and told them what Jesus had done" (John 11:45). The temple officers now realized that things were out of hand. They had to take decisive action. "So the chief priests and the Pharisees gathered the council, and said, 'What are we to do? For this man performs many signs. If we let him go on thus, every one will believe in him, and the Romans will come and destroy both our holy place and our nation'" (v. 47). Since the very existence of temple worship was at stake, a desperate plot was hatched. "So from that day on they took counsel how to put him to death" (v. 53).

This was not the first time that the life of the Lord had been sought, but it was the first time that the high priest sanctioned such a nefarious scheme. "But one of them, Caiaphas, who was high priest that year, said to them, 'You know nothing at all; you do not understand that it is expedient for you that one man should die for the people, and that the whole nation should not perish'" (v. 49). The issue was no longer *whether* Jesus should be put to death, but *when* and *how*.

Godly Jews received Jesus as Saviour, for they knew that his wisdom and power surpassed that of the prophets. But the temple officers put a radically different construction on the claims of the Lord. While pious Israelites were inquiring about the kingdom of heaven, the temple officers were murmuring with one another. Since Jesus claimed to be greater than Moses, the officers said he was guilty of driving a wedge between the system of temple worship and the people who supported it. They did not praise Jesus for his kindness and truth, for they did not measure virtue by these criteria. Rather than heeding the convictions of the heart, they took shelter under the ceremonies of the Mosaic law. The result was a dreadful misunderstanding. The more Jesus questioned the validity of ceremonial righteousness, the more he aroused resentment in those who rested in this righteousness.

Jesus was ready to explain his mission, thus lifting the misunderstanding. But the temple officers were too filled with

140

resentment to enter into friendly conversation. Hardness of heart blinded them to their opportunity.

The disciples were also puzzled by elements in Jesus' teaching, but they did not leave him on that account. Since they were held by the convictions of the heart, they could no more doubt the goodness of Jesus than they could doubt the evil of those who sought to kill him.

III

During the preparatory phase of his public ministry Jesus purposely drew the garments of obscurity about him. He not only vanished when the multitudes tried to make him king, but when he healed people he asked them not to reveal his identity. Jesus knew that if he yielded himself into the hands of sinners, he would be delivered up before his hour.

But the time had now come when the garments of obscurity had to be set aside, for it was written that the Messiah should be crucified openly. Jesus gained the needed fame by raising Lazarus from the dead. This was such a spectacular sign that reports of his power spread throughout Judea. When Jesus paid a final call at the home of Martha and Mary, he was the object of no small curiosity. "When the great crowd of the Jews learned that he was there, they came, not only on account of Jesus but also to see Lazarus, whom he had raised from the dead" (John 12:9).

Jesus made his triumphant entry into Jerusalem during the height of this fame. The multitudes were borne along by the convictions of the heart. They could not withhold praises from the man who, by word and deed, proved that he was the Messiah of God. The people gathered palm branches and went out to meet Jesus. They cried, "Hosanna! Blessed be he who comes in the name of the Lord, even the King of Israel!" (v. 13). The Apostle John specifically credits the raising of Lazarus for this extraordinary spectacle. "The crowd that had been with him when he called Lazarus out of the tomb and raised him from the dead bore witness. The reason why the crowd went to meet

141

him was that they had heard he had done this sign" (vv. 17-18).

John also tells how baffled the disciples were when they saw Jesus, the object of their hope, sitting on an ass's colt, accepting tributes which would eventuate in his trial and death. The contradiction was not lifted until the disciples looked back on the event, with the aid of the Holy Spirit. "His disciples did not understand this at first; but when Jesus was glorified, then they remembered that this had been written of him and had been done to him" (v. 16).

Jesus' triumphant entry put the chief priests and Pharisees in a very difficult position. Having acknowledged that Jesus possessed great power, they then had to decide whether this power came from God or Beelzebub. And since they suffered from hardness of heart, they promptly decided for Beelzebub. They argued that a true prophet would not question the traditions of the elders. And he certainly would not threaten the unity of God by claiming to be the Son of God.

When Jesus judged Israel by the law of God, he did more than impart information. He leveled an attack on the very foundations of ceremonial righteousness. This is why the temple officers had so little fellowship with his claims. When these officers saw their status in Israel disintegrate, a feeling of panic overtook them. In a frantic effort to stave off the threat of nonbeing, they determined to kill Jesus. And they did not care how they gained their end. They bribed Judas, and they bribed false witnesses. Finally, they outraged all sense of fair play by releasing Barabbas. The trial and death of Jesus brought tears to the eyes of pious Israelites, but the temple officers hailed it as a victory for God and righteousness.

Since Jesus knew that the temple officers would panic when they were stripped of power, he also knew that his own ministry would end in death. And by timing the manner in which he declared himself openly, he was able to time the very hour of his death. Jesus did not die as a martyr. He had power to lay down his life, and he had power to take it up again. His death was an offering, freely made — not a punishment, justly incurred.

IV

On one occasion Jesus asked a very critical question. "If I tell the truth, why do you not believe me?" (John 8:46). Jesus was warning his hearers against the leaven of pride. When a man senses no obligation to be bound by truth, he is free to accept whatever is congenial with personal interest. But he purchases his freedom very dearly. By surrendering his respect for truth, he separates himself from the living God, for God is a God of truth. A deceived man may have faith, to be sure, but his faith does not trace to sufficient evidences. He is a victim of illusions; his mind is prey to the demonic counsel of false prophets.

Therefore, when Jesus stood by the grave of Lazarus, he was conscious of his duty to create a body of evidences that would serve as an objective basis for faith. He knew that whatever else faith may be, it is at least a resting of the mind in the sufficiency of the evidences. Only truth has a right to command assent.

Before Jesus raised Lazarus, he took deliberate pains to acquaint the mourners with the source of his power. "And Jesus lifted up his eyes and said, 'Father, I thank thee that thou hast heard me. I knew that thou hearest me always, but I have said this on account of the people standing by, that they may believe that thou didst send me' " (John 11:41). Since many of the mourners could not draw near the entrance to the tomb, Jesus summoned Lazarus with a voice that could be distinctly heard by all. "When he had said this, he cried with a loud voice, 'Lazarus, come out.' " (v. 43). Jesus was preparing the mourners for the hour when they would bear witness to his Messianic office.

And when they did bear witness, they did not for a moment think they were judging a matter beyond their competence. After all, they had *seen* what Jesus did. If the raising of Lazarus was not an event that could be judged in the same way that an upright man judges any other event in history, then the senses

143

were no longer trustworthy and meaningful distinctions between fact and fiction could no longer be made.

Jesus' loud cry symbolizes the open character of the Christian religion. Everything necessary for salvation is revealed; nothing is reserved for a privileged caste. God expects no man to believe unless a body of sufficient evidences has been created. To submit to the claims of a false prophet is a culpable act, for it means that man senses no obligation to be bound by truth.

Critics often say that a person cannot become a Christian unless he surrenders his higher faculties. The critics, in this case, are wide of the mark. "It was a foul aspersion cast upon our religion by its ancient opposers, that it did require a mere belief, void of reason. . . . This suggestion, if true, were, I confess, a mighty prejudice against it, and no man indeed justly could be obliged to admit it upon such terms: but it is really a gross calumny; such a proceeding being disclaimed by the teachers and advocates of our religion, being repugnant to the nature and tenor thereof, being prejudicial to its interest and design, being contrary to its use and practice. Never any religion was indeed so little liable to the censure of obtruding itself on men's credulity, none ever so freely exposed itself to a fair trial at the bar of reason; none so earnestly invited men to scan and sift its pretences; yea provoked them for its sake and their own, upon most important considerations, (at the peril of their souls, as they tendered their own best advantage,) to a fair, discreet, careful examination thereof."[1]

V

Unless the heart is illuminated by the Holy Spirit, of course, it cannot come to a saving knowledge of Jesus Christ. It is manifestly wrong, therefore, to think that vital faith can be generated by the force of cleverly devised arguments. A sinner comes to Christ because he has been confronted by Christ. He trusts a living person, not a body of information.

[1]Isaac Barrow, *Theological Works*, Vol. IV, pp. 38-39.

But this does not mean that faith is a subjective leap which has no organic connection with information. On the contrary, a sinner confronts Christ in and through the Scriptures, and the Scriptures witness to a body of redemptive events that are as much a part of history as the voyage of Columbus.

The preparatory redemptive events are chronicled in the Old Testament. There was a time, not too long ago, when scholars questioned the authenticity of this chronicle. That time has now passed. Archaeology has made such strides that no careful student would deny that the account of God's dealings with Israel is a true account. There are gaps in the record, of course, but these gaps do not detract from the sufficiency of the evidences. The findings of archaeology are open for public inspection.[2]

Jesus not only accepted the historicity of the Old Testament, but he appealed to this history when he said that God had blessed the Jewish nation in a peculiar way. The Jews not only had laws which surpassed those of other nations, but they enjoyed covenantal assurances that God would send them a Saviour. Jesus drew on these assurances when he set forth his own Messianic claims. He said that *he* was the one of whom the prophets spoke when they described the future glory of Israel. And he had a valid reason for making this claim. He not only taught as one having authority, but he notarized his teaching with signs that could only be given by one who was uniquely related to God. On one occasion his hearers were constrained to ask, "When the Christ appears, will he do more signs than this man has done?" (John 7:31).

Critics, of course, are not happy with this. They wonder how we can be sure that Jesus gave the signs which are credited to him, for we have no external checks against these signs. Jesus foretold the destruction of Jerusalem and the founding of the church, and general history verifies the precision of these prophecies. But general history has nothing to say about the signs which Jesus gave. Or so it seems, at least.

2See Nelson Glueck, *Rivers in the Desert* (Farrar, Straus and Cudahy).

145

With the closing of one door, another opens before us. If there is no external testimony to support Jesus' claims, neither is there any countervailing testimony. The adversaries of the Lord did all they could to discredit his signs, but they did not deny the reality of the signs themselves. On the contrary, they admitted to one another, though not to outsiders, that Jesus did many mighty works. If they had tried to deny these works, they would have discredited themselves in the eyes of the very people they were trying to persuade; for these people had *witnessed* the Lord's power.

Though a reasonable opportunity was given to show that Jesus did not give the signs which were credited to him, this opportunity was never seized. Nor was this because Jesus went about in secret. "The miracles of Jesus were performed, for the most part, in an open and public manner, in the presence of multitudes of witnesses, under the inspection of learned and malignant enemies, in a great variety of circumstances, and for several years in succession."[3] If Jesus' adversaries could have denied the reality of his signs, they certainly would have done so.

This want of countervailing testimony not only serves as strong collateral evidence, but it is all that can reasonably be expected from those who would have worsened their own position by admitting more.

The early Christian apologists employed this argument when they disputed with the learned pagans. Neither Celsus, Hierocles, Porphyry, nor Julian denied that Jesus performed the miracles attributed to him. The pagans could only attempt to evacuate these miracles of Messianic force by assigning them to occult or magical power. This hypothesis was no different from that of the temple officers, and no more convincing.

A Christian never belittles the importance of miracles. He knows that valid faith traces to a body of sufficient evidences, and miracles help make up this sufficiency.

[3]Archibald Alexander, *Evidences of the Authenticity, Inspiration, and Canonical Authority of the Holy Scriptures,* p. 99.

Jesus asked men to believe him on the authority of his word alone, but he did not end his summons there. When he met people who were struggling with the forces of involuntary unbelief, he encouraged them to believe him for the sake of his works. He knew that the important thing was *faith,* not the route that faith took. Since people have different endowments, they are bound to be drawn by different levels of evidence. Miracles form one of these levels. They serve as proof that Jesus is Lord of the new creation. Therefore, when men believe Jesus for the sake of his works, they are confessing that he is the very Son of God.

VI

The New Testament tells about the ministry of Christ and the founding of the church. It develops a system which is consistent with itself, consistent with the Old Testament, and consistent with the facts of experience and history. The authors had nothing to gain, and much to lose, by setting down an orderly witness to Jesus' life, death, and resurrection. They never correct one another, nor is there any sign of collusion. They write in a personal, independent way, yet always with a loftiness and power that could only come from the Spirit of God.

Once again, critics are forward with objections. They argue that the claims of the New Testament cannot be tested by external standards. These claims, therefore, carry no more weight than those of any other religion. If we grant the rights of any one religion (so the objection goes), we operate on a principle that requires us to grant the rights of all religions. But this would lead to chaos, for religions contradict each other. A Christian has no right, therefore, to say that the New Testament rests on a body of sufficient evidences, and thus ought to be received. Religious claims are private and inward. They cannot be brought before the bar of human reason.

This argument sounds imposing, but it is specious from its inception. And every fair-minded person knows why. When we examine the claims of the New Testament, we offend good procedure if we impose criteria that are different in kind from those that we impose when *anything* meaningful is judged, whether in religion or out of it. For example, cultured people believe that Socrates was tried by an Athenian court. But why do they believe? They believe because they are satisfied with the sufficiency of the evidences. They not only presume that Plato was honest in reporting his facts, but no countervailing testimony has successfully called his report into question. Cultured people know that a rejection of sufficient evidences is a sign of incredulity. And incredulity is bad business, for by its refusal to proportion assent to evidence it leaves a person free to accept or reject whatever happens to suit him. This spells the end of all critical investigation.

A Christian realizes that it is difficult to tell what is meant by "the sufficiency of the evidences." But this difficulty is not peculiar to religion, or even to the Christian religion. The difficulty obtrudes whenever cultured people try to defend the reasons why they believe some things and not others.

A Christian is willing to accept the philosophy of evidences that men of ordinary intelligence accept when they go about their daily business. For example, such men believe that there was a man called Abraham Lincoln, and they believe because they feel that the evidences are sufficient. Historical claims are neither established nor refuted by science and philosophy. They can only be judged by the sort of common sense that takes pleasure in submitting to things as they are.

VII

Jesus satisfies the convictions of the heart as well as the demands of a critically disciplined intellect. These convictions serve as a fruitful point of contact between God and man. They are as objective as trees and rivers. If a man turns against them, he turns against reality itself.

When society spells out its moral philosophy, of course, it may never mention the convictions of the heart as such. But this in no way detracts from the universal persuasion that a man is good when he is kind and truthful.

If a person doubts the validity of this, let him explain why he trusts some people and not others. The answer is, some people are kind and truthful, while others are not.

The convictions of the heart not only tell us when a neighbor is good or evil, but they also tell us when a prophet is true or false. The validity of this can be established by the simplest experiment. Suppose a person stood in the streets and claimed to be a prophet of God. If he defended moral standards that were unfriendly with the convictions of the heart, we would know what to think of him. Our native concept of human dignity would force the issue. That it is evil to cheat and deceive; that children should obey their parents, and parents be kind to their children; that treachery and ingratitude are evil; that falsehood, theft, and murder have no place in a decent society — all of these, and any other persuasions belonging to the original constitution of man, draw on the same convictions that prompt a child to say that Cinderella is good, while her stepmother is evil. Unless the moral faculty is dulled by hardness of heart, a human being will be as prompt to credit kindness and truth as he will be to discredit unkindness and untruth. All conceivable wickedness traces to an offense against the convictions of the heart.

Since Jesus was always kind and truthful, he bears the mark of a true prophet. Truth *cannot* be called into being by an act of power. It is the property of a judgment (or the quality of an act) which accords with the real order of things. The convictions of the heart are part of this order, and Jesus accurately represented them.

Jesus defined an ethic that is final for all time, for there is no conceivable way in which an advance can be made on the law of love. Just as two and two make four, so kindness and truth make up the stuff of virtue. The second proposition is no less firmly grounded in reality, and no less entitled to be received, than the first.

If a demagogue appeared who advocated a spirit of revenge, who defended falsehood and barbarity, who attacked the institution of marriage, who urged men to defraud in their contracts, and who encouraged irresponsibility in political office, he would so offend the moral constitution of our nature, and so outrage the best interests of a decent society, that we would forthrightly reject him as an impious fraud. No new plea on his part would alter our opinion. We would have no fellowship with him because he would have no fellowship with the convictions of the heart.

If a person were to define the kind of a society in which he would want his children and his loved ones to live, he would find that he is defining the very ideals that form the kingdom of heaven. In other words, he is conceding that Christianity is friendly with the highest aspirations of the human heart. "There is no plan of benevolence, however exalted in its nature, or wide in its aim, in reference to which counsel may not be found in the Bible; there is no scheme projected for the promotion of human happiness, for the extension of liberty, for meliorating the condition of the downtrodden and oppressed, to which the principles of the Bible are not applicable; and there are no laws framed for the protection of human rights, for avenging wrong, for advancing the welfare of society, the germs or principles of which may not be found in the Bible, or which, in reference to purity, benevolence, or justice, are in advance of the principles laid down in the Word of God."[4] Civilized people have gradually overcome such barbarities as polygamy, infanticide, human sacrifice, slavery, and the injustices of a static social order. Moral improvements trace to the convictions of the heart, the same convictions that Jesus honored in his teachings and verified in his conduct.

[4]Albert Barnes, *Inquiries and Suggestions in Regard to the Foundation of Faith in the Word of God*, p. 107.

VIII

But Jesus did more than render a true account of the convictions of the heart. By the consistency of his own life he leveled a prophetic attack on the inconsistency of others. To receive Christ as Lord and Saviour, therefore, implies much more than assent to doctrine. It implies a vital act of repentance. We must be sincerely sorry for sin — the sin of not doing as we would be done by.

A word about human development will clarify what we mean. Every child is born with an intuitive sense of his own dignity. This dignity is the base from which the child measures degrees of good and evil in others. No matter what the little one may be taught in the home, down deep in his heart he knows that good people are kind and truthful, while evil people are not. This is proved in two separate ways. First, by the standards that the child uses when he quarrels; second, by the manner in which the child is able to enter the conflict between good and evil in a fairy tale. He finds the conflict so real that he identifies himself with those who are good. He wants good people to live happily ever after. He knows that if *they* do not count, then *he* does not count, and his heart will have none of that.

When we grow up, however, we are tempted to renounce our citizenship in the kingdom of love. If we yield to this temptation, we forfeit the wisdom of childhood. Pride says that a person is good when he is powerful, not when he is kind and truthful. When pride wins the day, we pervert the convictions of the heart by enlisting them in our quest for power. We use these convictions as criteria by which to measure faults in others, but not in ourselves. We know the truth (we condemn those who are unkind and untruthful), but we suppress the truth. Rather than being transformed by a knowledge of virtue, we draw comfort from observing that we are not as bad as others. Society is "very numerous of those who regulate their lives, not by the standard of religion, but the measure of other men's virtue; who lull their own remorse with the remembrance of

151

crimes more atrocious than their own, and seem to believe that they are not bad, while another can be found worse."[5]

When we are altogether honest with ourselves, we find that the flag of self-interest waves proudly over us. Even our defense of private property is subtly compounded with a zeal to gain an advantage over others.

Except for moments of prayer and contrition, everything in the historical self is tinctured by personal interest. Nothing is approved unless it clears with self-love.

Therefore, when Jesus says that no man is good, he is speaking a truth that is no less objective, and no less entitled to be received, than the axioms of geometry. Judged by the strict requirements of the law, all men *have* sinned and come short of the glory of God.

But men will not see and appreciate this truth unless they renew their covenant with the convictions of the heart. As long as they are content to heed the counsels of pride, they will continue to think more highly of themselves than they ought. This will not only deprive them of the wisdom that God gives to all who humble themselves, but it will make them indifferent to the connection between the kingdom of love and the kingdom of heaven. They will imagine that they can complete their lives without reference to divine grace; they will not ask the questions to which the gospel is the answer.

IX

When Jesus judges our imperfection, he does it with such compassion that he releases us from the fear that we must pretend to be better than we are. He assures us that if we will be honest with God, God will be gracious with us. And the moment we enter into a gracious relationship with God, we not only fall heir to the promises of the gospel, but we are also ready to accept our present duties in the kingdom of love.

With pride dethroned, we are able to accept a much more

[5]Samuel Johnson, *The Rambler*, No. 28.

modest concept of the self. We are delivered from the error of thinking that we must prove ourselves all the time. Kindness and truth become acceptable signs of status. Destructive anxiety cannot overwhelm us, for we are content to leave the work of salvation to God.

X

Since society is held together by interest and power, its standards of attainment are harshly competitive. And even worse, they are wickedly unjust, for they favor the rich and the powerful. One of the signs of the Messiah, therefore, was that he would preach the gospel to the poor. The poor have no status in society. They do not rank.

Jesus blessed the poor, for he himself was poor. He brought comfort to all who were cast down by a fear that they did not count. He assured them that they counted in the eyes of God, even though they did not count in the eyes of man. The gospel "brings peace into every bosom where it is cordially received. When the conscience is pierced with the stings of guilt, and the soul writhes under a wound which no human medicine can heal, the promises of the gospel are like the balm of Gilead, a sovereign cure for this intolerable and deeply-seated malady. Under its cheering influence, the broken spirit is healed and the burden of despair is removed far away. The gospel, like an angel of mercy, can bring consolation into the darkest scenes of adversity; it can penetrate the dungeon, and soothe the sorrows of the penitent in his chains, and on his bed of straw. It has power to give courage to the heart, and to brighten the countenance of the man who meets death on the scaffold or on the gibbet, if its precious invitations to the chief of sinners be sincerely embraced. It mitigates the sorrows of the bereaved, and wipes away the bitter tears occasioned by the painful separation of affectionate friends and relatives. By the bright prospects which it opens, and the lively hopes which it inspires, the darkness of the tomb is illumined; so that Christians are enabled, in faith of the resurrection of the body, to commit the remains of their dearest friends to the secure sepulchre, in confident hope that after a short sleep they will awake to life everlasting."[6]

The gospel is set forth on the testimony of sufficient evidences. But if pride hinders man from receiving this testimony, the fault lies with man himself — not with the gospel, not with the evidences, and not with the sincerity of the divine summons.

[6]Archibald Alexander, *op. cit.*, p. 218.

CHAPTER ELEVEN

The Way of the Cross Leads Home

"Brief life is here our portion,
Brief sorrow, short-lived care;
The life that knows no ending,
The tearless life, is there."
— Bernard of Cluny

When Jesus raised Lazarus from the dead, he did more than establish his own Messianic authority. He also clarified the nature of the kingdom of heaven. This kingdom will complete and fulfill the kingdom of love. It will be a fellowship from which all threats to happiness are forever banished. Death, the king of terrors, will be destroyed.

The Apostle John tells of the many wonderful things that believers can expect when they reach the kingdom of heaven. "God himself will be with them; he will wipe away every tear from their eyes, and death shall be no more, neither shall there be mourning nor crying nor pain any more, for the former things have passed away" (Revelation 21:3-4). No longing of the heart will be left unsatisfied.

I

Little children ask many questions about heaven. They want to know if the streets will really be made of gold. And how will we spend our time? Will we be able to fly through the air? But most of all, the children want to know how people will recognize one another. God will give us a resurrection body, to be sure, but what *kind* of a body? How old will we look? Some people die when they are young, while others live to a great age.

These questions are not only interesting in themselves, but they prove that a gentle heart will struggle with almost any problem rather than surrender its confidence that good people count in the eyes of God.

It *is* difficult to imagine what heaven will be like. But the difficulty is minor compared to what we face if death ends all. Nothing can be so dreadful as the prospect that our loved ones will perish like animals.

Jesus helps our infirmities by likening heaven to home. "Let not your hearts be troubled; believe in God, believe also in me. In my Father's house are many rooms; if it were not so, would I have told you that I go to prepare a place for you? And when I go and prepare a place for you, I will come again and will take you to myself, that where I am you may be also" (John 14:1-3). And what is home? Home is the place where love has its perfect way. It is a refuge from the competitive striving of a cruel and unfeeling society. At home we are accepted just as we are, without one plea.

This view of heaven has little scientific or philosophic value, of course. But it will satisfy the heart of a child, even as it will satisfy all who humble themselves and become like a child. A gentle person knows that if the kingdom of heaven fulfills and completes the kingdom of love, all else can be entrusted to Providence. God displaces our affection for the present world by giving us happy glimpses of the world that is to come.

The principle of displaced affections is eloquently illustrated by Thomas Chalmers. "Conceive a man to be standing on the margin of this green world; and that, when he looked towards it, he saw abundance smiling upon every field, and all the blessings which earth can afford, scattered in profusion throughout every family, and the light of the sun sweetly resting upon all the pleasant habitations, and the joys of human companionship brightening many a happy circle of society — conceive this to be the general character of the scene upon one side of his contemplation; and that on the other, beyond the verge of the goodly planet on which he was situated, he could descry nothing but a dark and fathomless unknown. Think you that he would bid a voluntary adieu to all the brightness and all the beauty that were before him upon earth, and commit himself to the frightful solitude away from it? Would he leave its peopled dwelling places, and become a solitary wanderer through the fields of non-entity? ... But if, during the time of contemplation, some happy island of the blest had floated by; and there had burst upon his senses the light of its surpassing glories, and its sounds of sweeter melody; and he clearly saw, that there, a purer beauty rested upon every field, and a more heartfelt joy spread itself among all the families; and he could discern there a peace, and a piety, and a benevolence, which put a moral gladness into every bosom, and united the whole society in one rejoicing sympathy with each other, and with the beneficent Father of them all. — Could he further see, that pain and mortality were there unknown; and above all, that signals of welcome were hung out, and an avenue of communication was made for him — perceive you not, that what was before the wilderness, would become the land of invitation; and that now the world would be the wilderness?"[1]

II

Scoffers dismiss the hope of heaven as an innocent but fruitless projection of wishful thinking. They grant that it would be *nice* to believe that good people have nothing to fear, but where is the evidence for this belief? Jesus has come and gone,

[1]From the sermon, "The Expulsive Power of a New Affection."

and things continue as they were from the beginning. Nature is a conflict between regular and irregular forces, society a conflict between justice and injustice. Therefore, would it not be better, let alone more honest, to make this world a happier place in which to live, rather than selfishly dreaming about heaven?

Indeed, we *should* do all we can to make this world a happier place in which to live, for love is dedicated to the task of relieving suffering. But unless love is joined by faith and hope, it cannot complete its mission. Love is an eternal tie; it draws on consolations that reach beyond the grave. Love says to the beloved, "You have nothing to fear, now or at any other time." Hence, the hope of heaven is not a sign of selfishness. It is a sign that love is being true to its own essence.

Jesus does not distribute photographs of heaven, nor does he satisfy the standards of science and philosophy. But he does satisfy the convictions of the heart, and he satisfies them with the highest of all possible evidences. Jesus *promises* an eternal home to all who trust him. What more could be asked?

Since the law of sin is actively at work in our members, we often promise more than we can make good. But Jesus faces no such prospect, for he is one in nature with the Father and the Holy Spirit. By his own resurrection from the grave he proved that he is Lord of the new creation.

III

Lazarus removed the garments of death and once again walked among the living. But Lazarus had nothing to say about the kingdom of heaven. He enjoyed no advantage over Martha and Mary; he continued to look to Jesus as the ground of his hope.

All Christians stand where Lazarus stood. They do not know why God was pleased to create a world into which such frightful things as illness and death should come. But they do know that God never intended to let illness and death have the last word.

158

And they know this because God has declared himself in the person of Jesus Christ.

When we become discouraged by the evils of the day, let us remember that Jesus gave his life with the express purpose of leading many sons into glory. As long as we are good, the evils of the day cannot harm us.

Science and philosophy will continue to boast of awesome achievements, but these achievements will neither add to nor subtract from the pleasure that a believer feels when God says, "I accept you; you count in my sight." Since our lives are hid with Christ in God, we have a reason for living and a reason for dying. "So we do not lose heart. Though our outer nature is wasting away, our inner nature is being renewed every day. For this slight momentary affliction is preparing for us an eternal weight of glory beyond all comparison" (II Corinthians 4:16-17).

IV

The Bible says that he who humbles himself will be exalted, and he who exalts himself will be humbled. This is a rule to which there is no exception. Now, if we are altogether honest with our own lives, we should not find it difficult to discover a reason for humbling ourselves. God has given many proofs that we are dependent creatures. A wise man will heed these proofs.

The death of Lazarus should remind us that only a few uncertain days separate us from such a state of putridity that even our dearest loved ones will banish us from their sight. Martha loved Lazarus, but she shrank before the odor of death. She wanted to keep a large stone between herself and her brother. The swift disintegration of the body is conclusive proof that man is a mystery unto himself. He is a mystery in life, and he is a mystery in death.

Every beat of the heart bears witness to our finitude. We are *not* the authors of our own existence. All our striving will prove futile in the end. Death will overtake us; our bodies will become food for worms.

159

This is why we must set our hope on God alone. When we are joined to Christ through faith and repentance, we are justified before the law and adopted into the family of God. The Lord then tells us that death is only a chamber in which we lay aside our earthly tabernacle with its pains and hindrances.

We were alone when we entered the world, but when we leave it we shall feel the abiding presence of the Lord. As death draws near and we dread the dark journey ahead, the Lord will assure us that our lives are precious in the sight of God. He will gently say, "Child, come home." Jesus has given his word that he will never leave us nor forsake us, and his word is as firm as his character.

"Therefore, my beloved brethren, be steadfast, immovable, always abounding in the work of the Lord, knowing that in the Lord your labor is not in vain" (I Corinthians 15:58).

INDEX

Abraham, 125
Adoption, 133ff., 160
Affections, 52, 127ff., 133, 156-157
Alcohol, 83-84
Anabaptist, 112
Anglicanism, 113-114
Anne Frank, 72-73
Anonymity, 84
Anxiety, 9, 11, 22, 57, 60, 78ff., 99
Apologetics, 7ff., 146
Archaeology, 145
Aristotle, 32, 40-41, 46
Arminian, 113
Atomic war, 29-30
Atonement, 11, 62-63, 88-89
Augustine, 7-8

Baptists, 115-116
Bethany, 54, 75-76, 78, 80, 86, 99-100, 108, 122
Bishop, 111-112
Blind man, 109-110
Body, 95-97, 101ff., 105, 156, 159
Boredom, 83
Brooding, 86-87
Butler, S., 56

Calvin, 113
Candide, 69
Cat, 37
Cemetery, 96
Centipede, 38-39
Chalmers, T., 90-91, 156-157
Charisma veritatis, 111
Child, 8-9, 12, 15ff., 20ff., 24ff., 28, 30-32, 36-38, 40-45, 48-49, 51, 53, 55ff., 67, 69, 71ff., 74, 84, 99, 102, 105, 110, 130, 133-134, 151, 156, 160
Christian Science, 68-69
Church, 110ff., 117ff.

Cinderella, 18, 26, 71, 73, 149
Communism, 30, 43
Congregationalists, 115-116
Confession (creed), 113, 116ff., 123, 137
Conservatives, 11, 107
Constructive anxiety, 87ff., 93
Convictions of the heart, 17ff., 20ff., 24-25, 27-28, 30ff., 35, 38, 40, 45, 51, 69, 70-72, 74-76, 95, 98-99, 102, 105, 131-132, 140-141, 148ff., 151-152, 158
Council of Trent, 118
Counter Reformation, 118

Daniel, 97
Darwin, 66, 75
Death, 13ff., 20-21, 34, 45, 55, 65-66, 71, 74, 80-81, 84, 89, 95-96, 98, 100, 104, 122-123, 138, 140, 142, 155, 158-160
Delinquent, 56ff.
Denomination, 115ff., 120-121
Destructive anxiety, 80ff., 85, 87ff., 93, 153
Detachment, 28ff., 31-32, 39ff., 43, 46-47, 49-50, 61, 73, 76, 95-96, 102, 104, 130, 134
Devotional self, 127ff., 132
Discipline, 57, 68, 88, 135-138
Displaced affections, 156-157
Dissenters, 114
Doctrine, 110ff., 117ff.

Elect, 113, 115
Elemental particles, 30-31
Enemies, 126-127, 139
Eucharist, 112
Euthyphro, 39-40
Evidences, 119, 124ff., 129-130, 133, 137, 139, 143ff., 148ff., 154, 157-158

161